The Selected Poems of Tu Fu

TRANSLATED BY DAVID HINTON

 A NEW DIRECTIONS BOOK

Grateful acknowledgment is made to the editors and publishers of *The American Poetry Review*, *The Literary Review* (special Chinese poetry issue), and *The New England Review/Bread Loaf Quarterly* in which some of these translations first appeared.

Thanks are also given to Columbia University Press for permission to quote, in the Translator's Notes, pp. 133–162, several excerpts from Burton Watson's translation of *The Complete Works of Chuang Tzu* (Copyright © 1968 Columbia University Press).

The map of "Tu Fu's China" facing the title page was prepared by J & R Art Services.

Manufactured in the United States of America
New Directions Books are printed on acid-free paper
First published clothbound and as New Directions Paperbook 675 in 1989
Published simultaneously in Canada by Penguin Books Canada Limited

Library of Congress Cataloging-in-Publication Data

Tu Fu, 712–770.
    [Poems. English. Selections. 1989]
    The selected poems of Tu Fu / translated by David Hinton.
      p.   cm.
    Bibliography: p.
    ISBN 0–8112–1099–5 (alk. paper). —ISBN 0–8112–1100–2 (pbk.)
    1. Tu Fu, 712–770—Translations, English.   I. Hinton, David,
1954–   .   II. Title.
PL2675.A24   1989
895.1'13—dc19

                                    88–38041
                                       CIP

New Directions Books are published for James Laughlin
by New Directions Publishing Corporation,
80 Eighth Avenue, New York 10011

THIRD PRINTING

CONTENTS

INTRODUCTION

Tu Fu lived from 712 to 770, during the illustrious High T'ang
literary period. In addition to being an unparalleled watershed
for Chinese poetry, it was a particularly infamous moment in
the country's political history, a moment of social upheaval
which determined the shape of Tu Fu's life and art. As his poems
are heavily dependent on the details of their biographical/his-
torical context, readers may want to read through the Biography
before beginning the poems themselves. It is designed so that
while reading the poems, a reader can easily place each poem in
the biographical narrative.

1. TU FU'S POETRY

The poet's transformation from craftsman to artist was perhaps
the most fundamental of many High T'ang innovations in poetry.
Singular artistic personalities emerged, culminating in the "ban-
ished immortal" Li Po made of himself, and in Tu Fu, the first
complete poetic sensibility in Chinese literature. Suffused from
the beginning with Confucian humanism, the Chinese poetic tra-
dition is essentially lyric and secular. It is a poetry of entirely
vulnerable and human dimensions, and Tu Fu remains its great
exemplar. He explored the full range of experience, and from
this abundance shaped the monumental proportions of being
merely human.

Tu Fu's inquiry was so comprehensive and original, in fact,
that it produced the poetic possibilities which came to define the
tradition. Although the radical innovations of his poetry denied

him recognition during his own lifetime, his work soon inspired such dissimilar poetics as Po Chü-yi's plain-spoken social realism and Meng Chiao's black, quasi-surreal introspection. And after the T'ang fell, the Sung's poetry of things at hand, with its composed simplicity, also found its source in Tu Fu. Indeed, his influence is so pervasive that China's poetic tradition can be located in terms of his work almost as readily as his work can be located in terms of it.

One dimension of Tu Fu's range is an objective realism unheard of in earlier poetry. He brought every aspect of public and private experience into the domain of poetry, including life's more unpleasant aspects, which traditional decorum had frowned upon. And the spirit of Tu's engagement with this unexplored terrain was profound in its implications: he conceived experience in the precise terms of concrete detail. As a result, the very texture of his poetry is an act of praise for existence itself.

Certain stereotyped hardships of the common people had long been treated indirectly in *yüeh-fu* ballads (p. 135), but Tu Fu was the first poet to write extensively about real, immediate social concerns. The devastating An Lu-shan rebellion, about which Tu Fu wrote relentlessly, was scarcely mentioned by Wang Wei, though he had a broader range than any poet before him and was as deeply affected by the rebellion as Tu Fu. And in his private poems, Tu found poetry in the most pedestrian experience. Such things as a poet's family and the small beauties and trials of ordinary life had scarcely appeared in Chinese poetry, and never in such a comprehensive, naturalistic way. But there is rarely such a clear distinction between the public and private in Tu Fu's poetry. Tu, who is known as the "poet-historian," lived at a particularly turbulent period in Chinese history, and few of his private poems are without social concerns. At the same time, his public poems rarely lack a private dimension. This dovetailing, in and of itself, was a substantial innovation in Chinese poetics, which traditionally required thematic unity.

Even during the High T'ang, poems were expected to address one topic while maintaining a single setting, mood, and tone. As these restrictions precluded the density his poetry required, Tu

Fu routinely shifted between thematic concerns while combin-
ing discontinuous moods, tones, images, perspectives, etc. In-
deed, he often juxtaposed these disparate elements within a sin-
gle couplet, the fundamental unit of Chinese poetry, radically
altering its traditional poise. Another strategy Tu Fu invented
to increase the complexity of his poems was the lyric sequence:
a series of lyrics not just grouped together, but closely inter-
woven to form a single long and complex poem (pp. 48, 81, 95).
His comprehensive sensibility also seems to explain Tu's rela-
tive lack of distinction in the 4-line quatrain form, and why his
most significant contributions to that form are three integrated
sequences (pp. 60, 63, 70).

In addition to a new world of objective clarities, Tu Fu's real-
ism opened up new depths of subjectivity, not only in terms of
subject matter, but formally as well. During his later years of
wandering, Tu's writing focused more and more on the solitary
self cast against the elemental sweep of the universe, and that
new subject matter was reflected in Tu's innovative language.
While the discontinuous organization continued to give his
poems a kind of intuitive complexity, Tu Fu's highly refined
language extended richness to the extreme, and beyond. It be-
came so distilled and distorted as to be nearly unintelligible at
times, while his imagery often approached the surreal. And in
his K'uei-chou poems, Tu also became the first Chinese poet to
exploit syntactic ambiguity in a calculated, generative way, often
with quite dissonant effects.

At first glance, Tu Fu's ceaseless worry over political affairs
may seem familiar to us, though extreme. As citizens of a demo-
cratic state, we live with the promise that we determine the gov-
ernment's policy, and we each suffer a peculiar grief of personal
responsibility for the abuses of "our" government. A scholar-
official in the Confucian order lived with a much greater promise
and responsibility because he belonged to the class whose very
raison d'être was to administer the government. And in Tu Fu's
case, the grief of implication was compounded by an almost
metaphysical sense of displacement which is quite foreign to us.
While a scholar-official's one proper place in the Confucian uni-

verse was helping the emperor care for the people, Tu briefly held only two governmental positions in his lifetime.

But a much deeper despair can be heard in the background of Tu Fu's poetry: the despair of a Confucian loss of faith. The human community was itself sacred and absolute in the Confucian order (its "religious" structure was manifest in a system of myth and ritual). By the end of his life, Tu had precious little reason for faith in that order. And without it, without civilization which was its full embodiment, nothing remained for him but an abyss— a metaphysical abyss come to life in the form of barbarian armies threatening to destroy China.

Nevertheless, there is at the heart of Tu Fu's sensibility a profound detachment from things, himself included. Rather than offering freedom from the mundane world, Tu's detachment is hopelessly complicated by a deep love for all things. While it allows his empathy to surpass the bounds of personal response, it also graces him with an exquisite sense of humor, one capable of subtly bringing a geologic perspective to even the most trying of his own circumstances.

In his later years, Tu Fu forged an identity of his life and art. His wandering in a decimated and increasingly foreign world became not just his predicament, but the human predicament. And the myriad details of his daily life became correlatives for the bones of exile which shape our spirit. He was a man of great wisdom speaking of an encounter with the extremes of our human experience, and in the measure of his voice even those extremes find repose.

2. CHINESE POETICS

All of the poems in this book are *shih*, the primary poetic form in the Chinese tradition. The basic structural unit of *shih* is the couplet. Individual lines are almost without exception end-stopped. End-rhymes occur in the second line of every couplet (and optionally in the poem's first line). Generally, a poem uses a single rhyme throughout, though in longer poems, the rhyme may shift, so that the poem will have several sections, each using its own rhyme. A caesura divides every line in a *shih*, almost always at the same place: after the second character in a 5-character line, and after the fourth character in a 7-character line.

Syntactically, *shih* poetry is classical Chinese pared to an absolute minimum. In fact, substantial amounts of the grammar are often absent. The resulting ambiguity is one of Chinese poetry's great strengths and beauties, especially as it is combined with the remarkably concrete nature of Chinese characters. This extreme reduction is facilitated by the seemingly monotonous and simplistic formal structure of *shih*. These two aspects of *shih* are bound together in a mutually supporting relationship: while the tight formal structure helps render the open syntax meaningful, the open syntax keeps the formal structure from becoming monotonous. Instead of monotony, the uniform structure gives the poem an underlying sense of balance and order.

During the High T'ang, the *shih* form could generally be divided along two axes. The first distinguishes between poems using a 5-character line and those using a 7-character line. In order to make this distinction clear in English, I have translated 5-character poems in quatrains and 7-character poems in couplets. The second axis distinguishes between ancient-style (*ku-shih*) and the recently developed modern-style (*chin-t'i-shih*). Ancient-style is the less rigorous of the two forms. Eight lines is one standard length for ancient-style poems, but they are frequently longer. And though they generally maintain a uniform line-length, exceptions are allowed. The primary forms of the highly regulated modern-style are the *lü-shih* (8 lines) and the *chüeh-chu* (4-line quatrains). The much less significant *p'ai-lü* has no length restrictions. In modern-style poetry, lines are without exception uniform in length, and the words making up every line must follow an elaborate tonal pattern, a kind of metrical equivalent to the parallel construction described below.

The two central couplets in a *lü-shih* must be parallel in construction (*chüeh-chu* may or may not employ parallel construction). That is, each word in the first line of a couplet must be paired in the second line with a word from the same semantic area, and the syntactic constructions of the two lines must mirror one another. The resulting contrasts and similarities between words and phrases create richly expressive relationships which are very important to a poem's field of meaning. A particularly good example is the second couplet of "Impromptu" (p. 75):

> (bank)
> sand   head / sleep egrets // gather fists / tranquil
>
> boat   tail / jump fish   // spread cut / cry(sound)
> (wake)

Throughout this couplet, the pairing of contrasting elements creates a sense of poise, which is the most basic function of parallelism. This balance of contrasts is uncomplicated in the first three positions (sand-boat, head-tail, sleep-jump). But in the fourth, a threatening tension arises when predator is coupled with prey, an impending violence already foreshadowed in the striking description of egrets as clenched fists in the first line (it is when reading the second line of a couplet that this added dimension of parallelism is registered). The tension builds through the fifth and sixth positions, and is released by the ambiguity in the couplet's final character: while a derivative meaning of *"ming"* is simply "sound," which accurately applies to the leaping fish, the written character is made up of the elements for mouth and bird, and its primary meaning is "a bird's cry." When read in its original sense, then, *"ming"* sets off the relentless life-and-death struggle of existence, shattering this peaceful scene (as well as the couplet's poise).

This is a remarkably expressive couplet, in which parallelism goes far beyond its basic function of holding the two lines together in a balanced relationship. Parallel construction creates another dimension in the poem, an interiority which is impossible to reproduce in English, although some of its effects can be rendered indirectly:

Serene

Flock of fists on sand—egrets asleep when
A fish leaps in the boat's wake, shivering, cry.

It is only because Chinese is such an austerely minimal language
that individual words have enough weight and immediacy for
these parallel interactions to occur. If a translator mimics paral-
lel structures in English, the very lines which are richest and
most intricate in the original become the most noticeably flat,
simplistic, and monotonous.

Poetry had traditionally been a social practice of the classi-
cally educated aristocracy. Its proper occasions were restricted
by convention, as were the form and subject matter considered
proper to any particular occasion. Although many of Tu Fu's
1,450 poems are occasional in the conventional sense, he came
to see virtually any human situation as the occasion of poetry.
At the same time, he superceded restrictions of formal category.
He was a master of all forms, and he employed each of them for
a wide variety of occasions and thematic concerns, the innova-
tive combinations giving poems new qualities of diction and tone.
A particularly good example of this is Tu Fu's innovative use
of the *lü-shih*, a form which developed during the T'ang Dy-
nasty. In his later years, after deciding to leave government ser-
vice and his homeland in the capital region, Tu Fu brought this
form to perfection. Prior to that decision, his major work was
written in a balance of forms tending toward ancient-style. After-
wards, in his devotion to the artistic discipline of poetry, he be-
came preoccupied with the technically demanding *lü-shih*, al-
most to the exclusion of the ancient-style. As ancient-style makes
the fewest formal demands on a writer, it was traditionally used
for more serious topics. The *lü-shih*, on the other hand, being so
extravagant in its formal demands, had generally been used as
a mere showcase for a poet's technical facility. Tu Fu was so
adept with the *lü-shih* form, however, that he could use it for
the most serious and demanding topics. The result not only gave
his late meditations an intricate elegance, but the parallel struc-

ture also added a new dimension to the poetic argument. Equally remarkable was Tu's extension of this form to poems on daily experience, both his own and that of peasants, gracing the commonplace with a striking beauty.

Because the qualities of tone and diction created as a poem's form interacts with its content can be significant, I have indicated form by using capital letters to begin lines in modern-style poems, and lower-case letters for those in ancient-style. As for the poetic language itself, however, I have made no attempt to render the distinction between them. The price paid would far outweigh the rewards.

Classical Chinese is a language quite distinct from spoken Chinese. It is a literary language defined by usage in the corpus of its standard texts, many of which were memorized by writers during their education. As a result, nearly every word and phrase is allusive in some sense. And Tu Fu was the most erudite poet in a tradition which expected poems to employ calculated allusion regularly. Generally, however, I have not tried to identify allusions unless they are essential to the poem's meaning. Although this eliminates a rich texture informing much of Tu Fu's poetry, and is the very nature of the language itself, to do otherwise would be a detailed scholarly endeavor having little to do with the translation of poetry.

3. TRANSLATION PRINCIPLES

My primary concern in these translations has been to recreate Tu Fu as a compelling poetic voice in English. To that end, I have freely used the resources available to contemporary English, though these resources share rather little with those of the High T'ang poetic language. The *shih* has so acutely distilled the extremely spare language of classical prose (to say nothing of the spoken language) that an equally reduced English would not be just uninteresting language, it would be virtually inarticulate. The language of *shih* is located, to a large extent, not in its *apparent* (written) elements, but in the reader. The knowledge, expectations, and conventions which the reader brings to a poem are so much a part of the language that even substantial areas of grammar are supplied in this way. In addition, a T'ang poem aspires to present the most concise sketch of its subject possible, and one fundamental convention is that the reader will take a very active role in creating the full picture in all its detail. Therefore, an extreme reduction in the *apparent* linguistic elements results in the most elegant and complex utterances in the language. English, on the other hand, is almost entirely manifest in its *apparent* language, which is why Chinese can appear so clear and simple when seen from the perspective of English. The characteristics required by English are altogether unlike those required by Chinese. Eloquence in English demands language which has *apparent* intricacy, variety, subtlety, drama, and a form of rhythm and music which is qualitatively different from that of Chinese.

So, although I have tried to remain faithful to the content of Tu Fu's poems, I have made little attempt to mimic the formal or linguistic characteristics of the originals, because to do so would be to misrepresent them entirely. The configuration of characteristics which defines the Chinese poetic language is so fundamentally different from that of contemporary English that individual characteristics (some of which are shared) cannot have the same value in both systems. My overall intent has been to create reciprocal configurations in English. And rather than resolving the uncertainties of the originals, I have tried to re-create Tu Fu's poems as new systems of uncertainty, as the poems he might have written had he been writing in today's English.

*

Tu Fu's years of wandering did not end with his death. Because of the poverty and dislocation of his family, he was not finally buried in the family graveyard near Lo-yang until his grandson managed to arrange it in 813, forty-three years after his death. Although Tu's work had aroused relatively little interest during his lifetime, the praise in Yüan Chen's tomb inscription indicates that his poems had begun to startle and move readers. Thus, he satisfied the terms of his famous statement on poetics: "If my words aren't startling, death itself is without rest." My hope for these translations is that they might deepen Tu's millennial repose.

Vermont, January 1989   David Hinton

My Thanks

To Jody Gladding for advice during the revisions, support, and
    much more;
To Eliot Weinberger for his help with the manuscript and his
    indispensable spirit;
To J. P. Seaton for support and for reading the first draft;
To New Directions and Peggy Fox, my editor;
And, for financial assistance, to Cornell University, The Ludwig
    Vogelstein Foundation, The Pacific Cultural Foundation, and
    The Pennsylvania Council on the Arts.

No one knows your thoughts, master,
And night is empty around us, silent.

EARLY POEMS

GAZING AT THE SACRED PEAK

For all this, what is the mountain god like?
An unending green of lands north and south:
from ethereal beauty Creation distills
there, *yin* and *yang* split dusk and dawn.

Swelling clouds sweep by. Returning birds
ruin my eyes vanishing. One day soon,
at the summit, the other mountains will be
small enough to hold, all in a single glance.

VISITING FENG-HSIEN TEMPLE AT LUNG-MEN

I leave the temple, but stay another
night nearby. The dark valley all empty
music, moonlight scatters lucid
shadow among trees. Heaven's Gap

cradles planets and stars. I sleep
among clouds—and stirring, my clothes
cold, hear the first bell sound
morning for those waking that deeply.

WRITTEN ON THE WALL AT CHANG'S HERMITAGE

In spring mountains, alone, I set out to find you.
Axe strokes crack—crack and quit. Silence doubles.

I pass snow and ice lingering along cold streams, then,
Late light wavering at Stone Gate, enter these woods.

Deer graze here each morning, for you harm nothing.
And because you want nothing, auras of silver and gold

Grace nights. Facing you *on a whim* in bottomless dark, the way
Here lost—I feel it drifting, this whole empty boat.

THOUGHTS, FACING RAIN:
I GO TO INVITE HSÜ IN

Clouds summit above T'ai Mountain, peak
And summit, serene as full-river voices
In vacant space. Lightning skitters swallows
On painted screens. Fish dip back below

Steady rains, deepen and drift. When I
Hear you outside, I am drinking cheap wine.
Ashamed of mud, calling *Bring your horse
Right up to the porch here*, I invite you in.

FOR LI PO

Autumn returns, and again we are cast thistledown together
On the winds. The elixir of immortality has eluded us—

Ko Hung must be ashamed. Days drunk and singing too loud,
Given to the wind, yet resolute—so brave, and for whom?

CH'ANG-AN I

A LETTER FROM MY BROTHER AT LIN-YI ARRIVES LAMENTING RAINS AND FLOODING ON THE YELLOW RIVER. AS ASSISTANT MAGISTRATE, HE IS WORRIED ABOUT THE COLLAPSING DIKES, SO I SEND THIS POEM TO EASE HIS THOUGHTS

The Dual Principles have ended in rain and wind,
Billows and waves falling from a hundred
Mountain valleys. I hear the river is broken
Wide open and gathering every distance into one

Cold rising sea. Lament seizes every district.
Officials grow quiet with worry. And directing
Defenses against the river, you are also
Helpless. Your foot-long letter arrives, saying

There isn't time for new dikes. Enlisting
Mu Wang's turtles and crocodiles is impossible,
And looking to magpies from the Celestial River
Futile. South of Yen, farmlands are nothing

Now but wind. Even Chi hills are no more
Than sunken thistleweed. Waters thick with
Clams and snails lap at city walls; hornless
Dragons and dragons with scales roam every pool.

Hsü Pass deep as any water god's palace,
Chieh-shih Mountain a mere tip of autumn hair,
Nothing remains of peasant villages but a lone
Tree and ten-thousand boats lost in azure sky.

Adrift, slight as a flood-charm, I sail for peach
Branches of immortality. There, at the edge of
Heaven with my fishhook and line, surely
I will land the P'eng-lai tortoise for you.

SONG OF THE WAR-CARTS

War-carts clatter and creak,
horses stomp and splutter—
each wearing quiver and bow, the war-bound men pass.
Mothers and fathers, wives and children—they all flock
alongside, farewell dust so thick Hsien-yang Bridge
disappears. They get everywhere in the way, crying

cries to break against heaven, tugging at war clothes.
On the roadside, when a passerby asks war-bound men,
war-bound men say simply: *Our lots are drawn often.*
Taken north at fifteen, we guard the Yellow River. Taken
west at forty, we man frontier camps. Village elders
tied our head-cloths then. And now we return, our
hair white, only to be sent out again to borderlands,

lands where blood swells like sea-water. And Emperor Wu's
imperial dreams of conquest roll on. Haven't you heard
that east of the mountains, in our Han
                                homeland, ten hundred towns and
ten thousand villages are overrun by thorned weeds,
that even though strong wives keep hoeing and plowing,
you can't tell where crops are and aren't? It's worst for
mighty Ch'in warriors: the more bitter war they outlive,
the more they are herded about like chickens and dogs.
Though you are kind to ask, sir,
how could we complain? Imagine
this winter in Ch'in. Their men
still haven't returned, and those
clerks are out demanding taxes.

Taxes! How could they pay taxes?
Even a son's birth is tragic now.
People prefer a daughter's birth,

a daughter's birth might at least end in marriage nearby.
But a son's birth ends in an open grave who knows

where. You haven't seen how bones from ancient times
lie, bleached and unclaimed along the shores of
Sky-Blue Seas—how the weeping of old ghosts is
joined by new voices, the gray sky by twittering rain.

CROSSING THE BORDER

1

So far from my village—sent so far
away to the Chiao River. Reporting
dates are final, and nets of calamity tangle
anyone who resists. Our lands are rich

enough and more for a king, what good
can a little more ground bring?
Shouldering my spear, lost, parents'
love lost—tasting silence, I go.

2

I left home long ago. Now, the early
abuse is over. My bones a father's love,
my flesh a mother's—how are they so
broken in a son still alive to guess at

his death (shaking free of its reins,
a horse tearing blue silk from my hands, or
after inching down a mountainside, eighty
thousand feet, trying for a fallen flag)?

3

In a river of muted cries, I sharpen
my sword, longing for the heart's
silence long laced with cries of stricken
people. But the water bleeds, the edge

cuts my hand. Once devoted to his
country, what has a good man to resent?
Heroes live forever in Unicorn Pavilion,
and the bones of war rot quickly away.

4

Always some clerk to scare-up men and
send them out. The frontiers are well-
supplied. Death certain as life,
we advance. And still, officers rage.

Meeting a friend on the road, I send
letters home. . . . O, how are we cast so
far from one another, broken apart, never
to scrape by in sorrow together again?

5

Distant, ten thousand miles and more
distant, they take us to join vast armies.
Soldiers come to joy and grief by chance,
how could generals hear everything? Riders

appear across the river. Then suddenly
they arrive, ten hundred Mongol brigades.
From this rankless beginning, how long
until my reputation is made and confirmed?

6

In drawing bows, draw the strongest;
in using arrows, use the longest.
To shoot men, first shoot their horses;
to take enemies, first take their generals.

But killing must be kept within limits:
a country is nothing without borders. Far
beyond any claim of defense, what is ours
now with all this slaughter and death?

7

Pushing our horses hard through mixed
rain and snow, we enter high mountains.
The trail narrows. Our fingers breaking
through layers of ice, we hug frozen rock.

So far from our Chinese moon,
building walled forts—will we ever
return? At dusk, clouds drift away
south, clouds I cannot mount and ride.

8

The Mongols descend on our positions.
For hundreds of miles, dust-filled
winds darken skies. A few brave
sword strokes drive armies before us.

We capture their famed chieftain and
present him, tied by the neck, when
we return. Preparing to march, we stand
in formation. One win—so much talk.

9

In ten years and more at war, how could I
avoid all honor? People so treasure it,
I thought of telling my story, but sounding
like all the others would be too shameful.

War flickers throughout our heartland
and rages steadily along the frontiers.
With such fine men chasing ambition
everywhere, who can elude savage beggary?

NEW YEAR'S EVE AT TU WEI'S HOME

The songs over pepper wine have ended.
Friends jubilant among friends, we start
A stabled racket of horses. Lanterns
Blaze, scattering crows. As dawn breaks,

The fortieth year passes in my flight toward
Evening light. Who can change it, who
Stop it for even a single embrace—this dead
Dazzling drunk in the wings of life we live?

MEANDERING RIVER:
THREE STANZAS, FIVE LINES EACH

1

Meandering River desolate, autumn skies deep—withered
bits of blown lotus and chestnut drift. Lamenting this

wanderer handed-down into old age is empty: White
pebbles and shoreline sand also chafe back and forth.
A wailing swan, alone, cries out in search of its kind.

2

Singing that which occurs, neither modern nor ancient,
my rising song only breaks against bushes and trees.
And those houses stand, in their lavish parade, countless.

I welcome this heart of ash. Dear brother, dear little
niece—why so hurt, why these tears falling like rain?

3

I have asked enough answers of heaven for one life.
Enough, having hemp and mulberry fields there,

to settle near South Mountain, in Tu-ling. Riding
with Li Kuang, in simple clothes, I will end my
failing years shooting phantom tigers as they appear.

LI STOPS BY ON A SUMMER DAY

In distant woods, summer heat thin,
you stop by. It could be in a village
somewhere, my little tumbledown
house near the city's south tower—

neighbors open and simple-hearted,
needs easily filled. Call across
for wine, the family to the west
gladly hands a pot over the fence,

fresh, unstrained. We spread mats
beside the stream. Clear winds arrive
carelessly, and you imagine autumn
stunning already. Everywhere, nesting

birds bicker, thickening cicada songs
fill lush leaves—who calls my home
among this racket of things secluded?
We linger out flawless, dusk-tinted

blossoms on water—a world enough now,
enough and more. And without worry,
the winepot still far from empty, I go
again with schemes aplenty for more.

9/9, SENT TO TS'EN SHEN

I step out for a moment, then back.
Foundering rain-clouds haven't changed;
ditchwater babbles everywhere. Thinking
of you, I grow thin. I mutter songs

on the west porch. Meals pass indistinct
as night and day. Meandering River a mere
half-step away—and yet, meeting you
there is impossible now. . . . How much

more must earth's simple people bear?
Their farms are beyond hope. And if we
scold the cloud-spirit, who will ever
patch these leak-sprung heavens? O,

sun and moon lost to a haze and waste
world, twitter and howl. Noble men
driven into twisted paths, simple-hearted
people, frantic, run themselves ragged.

Even the exalted South Mountain might
already have sunk and drifted away.
What is it for—here at my eastern fence,
this holiday confusion of chrysanthemums?

Your new poems? Our shared weakness
for wine? Cut them—I'll cut the yellow-
bloomed things and fill my sleeves
far too beautifully for nothing today.

AUTUMN RAIN LAMENT

Looming rain and reckless wind, an indiscriminate
ruins of autumn. The four seas and eight horizons all

gathered into one cloud—you can't tell an ox coming
from horse going, or the muddy Ching from clear Wei.

Wheat-ears are sprouting on the stalk, and millet-
clusters turn black. Nothing arrives from farmers,

not even news. Here in the city, quilts bring
one handful of rice. No one mentions old bargains.

FENG-HSIEN RETURN CHANT

An old man from Tu-ling unhinged a life
in twisted thought and harlequin rags
begging to rescue the times like any fool,
as if he were Chi or Chieh. He will end

empty as Hui Tzu's huge, useless gourd.
A white-haired man too willing to suffer,
once my coffin is covered, this longing for
what will suffice will end. And yet,

it is poverty's year. I mourn the people,
my song brimmed with lament, to my aging
schoolmates' amusement—a held sigh
and fever of the heart. Not that I haven't

a hermit's love for rivers and seas,
for a life wind scatters in vanishing
days and months, but with a ruler rare as
Yao or Shun, I couldn't endure that

endless farewell. We have everything
good government could possibly want now
but good government. The sunflower
cannot change what it is, it will always

turn toward the sun. And the frenzied ant
searching for its snug little burrow,
how could it ever be a huge whale
taking comfort in the boundless sea?

It's the nature of things. What a fool
I've been, taking my concerns around on
polite visits—so determined, so very
willing to drown myself in this dust.

Ch'ao and Yu refused to abandon their
hermit's discipline. In shame before them,
drinking recklessly, I lose myself chanting
songs to conjure broken sorrows away.

The hundred grasses in tatters, high wind-
scoured ridges and stars—it is year's end
on the imperial highway. Among shadows
towering in the heart of night, I set out.

Soon, fingers frostbitten, I can't tie my coat
closed when it falls open. Among peaks I pass
in the bitter morning, on Li Mountain, our emperor
sleeps soundly. Ch'ih Yu banners trail out

into stars. In this cold, empty canyon passing
armies have polished smooth, steam billows
over his little Jasper Lake. Constellations
chafe and jar against his imperial lances.

Regal ministers were up late taking their
pleasure here. Music swelling to echo
through canyons, not a poor man in sight,
they were bathed by their choice women,

women pampered with silks that come slowly
from the hands of shivering farm wives. Their
husbands are horsewhipped by tax collectors
come demanding tributes for the palace,

and our wise king, wishing his people well,
sends baskets and bushels full of sincere
gifts. With trusted ministers without principles,
why squander perfectly good supplies?

The number of august men dawn brings to court
frightens any decent man. Even the emperor's
imperial-gold tableware, they say, has been
divvied-out among blue-blooded families.

In the central hall, incense lilts from jade-
white bodies of dancing goddesses. Sable coats
warm, a grieving flute harmonizing with clear
pure *koto* songs, guests savor camel's hoof

soup, fragrant whipped kumquats, frosted
coolie oranges. . . . The imperial-red gate:
dumped wine and meat rank inside, the frozen
dead by the road outside. All and nothing

Here but a key and half-step different. How
could such misery endured ever be retold?
I turn north toward the Wei and Ching.
At the flooded ferry-landing, I turn again.

A seaful of water flooding from the west looms
and summits to the edge of sight, and beyond—
to K'ung-t'ung Mountain peaks. Once it wrecks
the pillars of heaven, will anything remain?

One bridge is still holding, its welcome
trestlework a creaking howl and whisper
in wind. The current flowing broad and wild,
travelers manage to help each other across.

My dear wife keeping wind and snow from our
family in a strange place. . . . How could I
leave them so long alone? Thinking we would
at least be together again going without,

I come home to the sound of weeping, wailing
cries for my little son, stone-dead now of hunger.
The neighbors sob in the street. And who am I
to master my grief like some sage, ashamed

even to be a father—I, whose son has died
for simple lack of food? A full autumn
harvest—how could I have known, how
could the poor still be so desperate with want?

Son of an untaxed family, never dragged off
to make someone's war, I have lived a life
charmed, and still too sad. O, the poor
grieve like a boundless wind in autumn trees.

Those who have lost all for war wander
darkly in my thoughts. Distant frontiers . . .
The elusive engines of grief loom like
all South Mountain, heave and swing loose.

CH'ANG-AN II

MOONLIT NIGHT

Tonight at Fu-chou, this moon she watches
Alone in our room. And my little, far-off
Children, too young to understand what keeps me
Away, or even remember Ch'ang-an. By now,

Her hair will be mist-scented, her jade-white
Arms chilled in its clear light. When
Will it find us together again, drapes drawn
Open, light traced where it dries our tears?

CH'EN-T'AO LAMENT

Now fine homes in ten prefectures have dead sons
making water with their blood on Ch'en-t'ao Marsh.

An early winter's panoramic waste: crystal sky,
the silence of war. Forty thousand dead in a day.

Mongol battalions return. Their arrows bathed blood-
black, drunk in the markets, they sing Mongol songs.

And we face north to mourn, another day conjuring
our army's appearance passing into hopeful night.

FACING SNOW

Enough new ghosts now to mourn any war,
And a lone old grief-sung man. Clouds at
Twilight's ragged edge foundering, wind
Buffets a dance of headlong snow. A ladle

Lies beside this jar drained of emerald
Wine. The stove's flame-red mirage lingers.
News comes from nowhere. I sit here,
Spirit-wounded, tracing words onto air.

SPRING LANDSCAPE

Rivers and mountains survive broken countries.
Spring returns. The city grows lush again.
Blossoms scatter tears thinking of us, and this
Separation in a bird's cry startles the heart.

Beacon-fires have burned through three months.
By now, letters are worth ten thousand in gold.
My hair is white and thinning so from all this
Worry—how will I ever keep my hairpin in?

THINKING OF MY LITTLE BOY

Apart still, and already oriole songs
Fill warm spring days. Changing seasons
Startle me here without you, my little
Sage. Who talks philosophy with you now?

Clear streams, empty mountain paths, our
Simple village home among ancient trees . . .
In grief thinking of you, sleep: sunning
On the veranda, I nod off beneath blue skies.

ABBOT TS'AN'S ROOM, TA-YÜN MONASTERY

The lamp gutters and flares. Sleepless,
the scent of incense delicate, my mind
exacts clarity. In these depths of night,
the temple looming, a windchime shudders.

Blossoms veiled in heaven's dark, earth's
clarity continues—fragrant, secretive.
Jade String floats out beyond the roof, cut
where the temple phoenix wheels and soars.

Sutra chants drift from the hall. A bell
sounds, lingering, resounding over the bed.
Soon, dawn breaking across fertile plains,
I will face brown dust and sand, and grieve.

P'ENG-YA SONG

I remember long ago slipping away
in precarious depths of night. The moon
bright on Po-shui Mountain, I eluded
rebel armies and fled with my family

far north by foot on P'eng-ya Road.
By then, most people we met had lost all
shame. Scattered bird cries haunted
valleys. No one returned the way we came.

My silly, starved girl bit me and screamed.
Afraid tigers and wolves might hear,
I cradled her close, holding her mouth,
but she squirmed loose, crying louder still.

Looking after us gallantly, my little boy
searched out sour-plum feasts. Of ten days,
half were all thunder and rain—mud
and more mud to drag ourselves through.

We didn't plan for rain. Clothes ever
colder, the road slippery, an insufferable
day's travel often took us but a few short
miles by nightfall. Wild fruit replaced

what little food we had carried with us.
Low branches became our home. We left dew-
splashed rocks each morning, and passed
nights at the smoke-scored edge of heaven.

We had stopped at T'ung-chia Marsh,
planning to cross Lu-tzu Pass, when you
took us in, Sun Tsai, old friend, your
kindness towering like billowing clouds.

Dusk already become night, you hung lanterns
out and swung door after door wide open.
You soothed our feet with warm water
and cut paper charms to summon our souls,

then called your wife and children in, their
eyes filling with tears for us. My chicks
soon drifted away in sleep, but you brought
them back, offering choice dishes of food.

You and I, you promised, will be forever
bound together like two dear brothers.
And before long, you emptied our rooms,
leaving us to joy and peace and rest.

In these times overrun with such calamity,
how many hearts are so open and generous?
A year of months since we parted, and still
those Mongols spin their grand catastrophes.

How long before I've grown feathers and wings
and settled beside you at the end of flight?

JADE-BLOSSOM PALACE

Below long pine winds, a stream twists.
Gray rats scuttle across spent rooftiles.
Bequeathed now beneath cliffs to ruin—who
knows which prince's palace this once was?

Azure ghostflames flood shadow-filled rooms.
Erosion guts manicured paths. Earth's
ten thousand airs are the enduring music,
autumn colors the height of indifference.

All brown earth now—the exquisite women
gracing his golden carriage have all become
their rouge and mascara sham. Of those
stately affairs, one stone horse remains.

Sitting grief-stricken in the grasses,
I sing wildly, wiping away tears for life
scarcely passes into old age, and no one
ever finds anything more of immortality.

THE JOURNEY NORTH

Heaven and Earth are racked with ruin,
sorrow and sorrow, no end in sight.

Slowly, roads and haphazard lanes pass.
Chimney smoke rare, cold wind merely
drones on. All we meet are moaning
wounded, bleeding still and muttering.

I turn to watch flags and streamers over
Feng-hsiang flare up at dusk and smother,
then climb through foothills and cold
hollows where cavalries stopped for water.

The fields of Pin spread falling away
into lowlands halved by the raging Ching,
and the savage tiger we come upon
splits gray cliffs apart with its roar.

Chrysanthemums scatter autumn petals
across stone scarred by ancient war-carts.
And soon, clouds in clear sky shape ethereal
joy. O, how quiet things apart contrive

delight, even now. Slight jewels tossed
among acorns and chestnuts, mountain
berries have ripened to rich cinnabar reds,
blacks deeper than lacquered bits of night.

What falling rain bathes is weighted,
whether bitter or sweet, with fruit.
Here, my Peach Blossom nostalgia fills with
remorse for life's simplicity squandered.

From upper slopes, I look out across cliffs
breaking from disappearing valleys, to Fu-chou
highlands—then hurry, making the river
before my servant can leave ridgeline trees.

Owls call from mulberries turning yellow.
Ground squirrels, hands folded, stand about
their burrows. Soon, in the gaping night,
we cross battlefields of moonlight chilling

white bones. Warriors at T'ung-kuan Pass—
how quickly millions scattered into the past
there. And half the people followed, broken
Ch'in people mauled into strange other things.

And I, fallen also among the Mongol dust,
I return after a year to our thatched home,
a queer sight of white hair, finding my family
graced with countless mends and patches.

In hushed litany with pine winds, a mourning
brook shares our sobs. All that time
pampered, all my delight—my little
son wears a face whiter than snow now.

Seeing his father, not even socks for his
dirt and grime feet, he turns away and cries.
In skirts sewn and pieced just to cover
their knees, our two girls keep near my bed.

Patchwork seascapes of billows and torn
waves, their little cloaks are skewed
odds and embroidered ends, a purple-phoenix
potpourri among topsy-turvy sea gods.

An old man, heartsick, worried and driven
into bed vomiting and shitting for days—*but
I did manage a bag of silks for you, didn't I?
No more shivering from the cold, at least.*

Powder and mascara, too, the fine, frail
wrappers untied, and quilts laid out gingerly.
My poor, thin wife is all bright-eyed again.
Her madcap girls merrily comb at their hair.

Elfin studies of their mother, leaving nothing
undone, they smear dawn make-up around with wild
abandon. Soon rouge is plastered everywhere,
and they are painting on demon-thick eyebrows.

Returned large as life to my girls and boys,
they nearly forget their hunger asking
questions, bickering, tugging at my poor beard.
How could I scold them? Buffeted still

in the grief warring rebels spawn, I savor
all this racket, this clamoring around.
Tomorrow's want looming, and I scarcely
returned to comfort them, what could I say?

MEANDERING RIVER

1

Spring diminished with each petal in flight, these
Ten thousand wind-tossed flakes overwhelm me with grief.

Now the last blossoms are passing before my eyes
(All that anguish), I can't afford to scrimp on wine.

Kingfishers nest in small, lakeside pavilions. Beside
Stately tombs at the park's edge, unicorns lounge.

Joy is the nature of things. Look closely—where is
This fleeting consequence you've tangled your life in?

2

Day after day, I pawn spring clothes when court ends
And return from the river thoroughly drunk. By now,

Wine debts await me wherever I go. But then, life's
Seventy years have rarely ever been lived out. And

Shimmering butterflies are plunging deep into blossoms
Here. Dragonflies quavering in air prick the water.

Drift wide, O wind and light—sail together
Where we kindred in this moment will never part.

DREAMING OF LI PO

Death at least gives separation repose.
Without death, its grief can only sharpen.
You wander out in malarial southlands,
and I hear nothing of you, exiled

old friend. Knowing I think of you
always now, you visit my dreams, my heart
frightened it is no living spirit
I dream. Endless miles—you come

so far from the Yangtze's sunlit maples
night shrouds the passes when you return.
And snared as you are in their net,
with what bird's wings could you fly?

Filling my room to the roof-beams, the moon
sinks. You nearly linger in its light,
but the waters deepen in long swells,
unfed dragons—take good care old friend.

FOR THE RECLUSE WEI PA

Lives two people live drift without
meeting, like Scorpio and Orion,
without nights like this: two friends
together again, candles and lamps

flickering. And youth doesn't last.
Already gray, we ask after old friends,
finding ghosts—everywhere, ghosts.
It startles the heart, and twists there.

Who dreamed it would be twenty years
when I left? You weren't married then,
and look—already a proper little
flock of sons and daughters. In gleeful

respect for their father's friend, they
ask where I've come from. And before
the asking and telling end, they are
bundled off to help with soup and wine,

spring scallions cut fresh in evening rain,
steamed rice garnished with yellow millet.
Pronouncing reunions extinct, you pour
ten cups a throw *to our health*. Ten cups,

and I'm drunk on nothing like your unfailing
friendship. Tomorrow, between us in all
this clamor of consequence, mountain
peaks will open out across two distances.

THE CONSCRIPTION OFFICER AT SHIH-HAO

It was late, but out in the night
when I arrived, he was collaring men.
Her husband, the old inn-keeper, slipped
over the wall, and she went to the gate.

The officer cursed loud and long, lost in
his rage. And lost in grief, an old woman
palsied with tears, she began offering
regrets: *My three sons left for Yeh.*

Then finally, from one, a letter arrived
full of news: two dead now. Living
a stolen life, my last son can't last,
and those dead now are forever dead and

gone. Not a man left, only my little
grandson still at his mother's breast.
Coming and going, hardly half a remnant
skirt to put on, she can't leave him

yet. I'm old and weak, but I could hurry
to Ho-yang with you tonight. If you'd
let me, I could be there in time,
cook an early meal for our brave boys.

Later, in the long night, voices fade.
I almost hear crying hush—silence. . . .
And morning, come bearing my farewells,
I find no one but the old man to leave.

PARTING IN OLD AGE

Vanished in all four directions—peace,
peace old age will never bring. My
sons and grandsons all war-dead,
why live this body's life out alone?

Tossing my cane aside, I set out, pitiful
sight even to fellow soldiers—a man
lucky to have these few teeth left
now the marrow is dried from his bones.

Among armor-clad warriors, I offer
deep farewell bows to the magistrate,
and my dear wife lies by the roadside
sobbing, her winter clothes worn paper-

thin. This death's farewell wounds me
again with her bitter cold. From this,
no return. And still, she calls out
behind me: *You must eat more—please.*

T'u-men's wall is strong, Hsing-yüan
ferry formidable. It's not like Yeh.
Though no less certain, death won't come
suddenly. Life is separation and return,

is plentiful one day, and the next
withered. It is the nature of things, I
know, but thinking of our shared youth,
I look back slowly, heart-stricken.

Nothing in ten thousand kingdoms but war.
Beacon-fires smother ridges and peaks.
Grasslands and forests reeking of the dead,
Blood turns brooks and springs cinnabar-red.

Not an untormented village left anywhere,
how can I hesitate, how avoid this life
torn loose from my calm, thatched-home
life laying my insides out bare to ruin.

CH'IN-CHOU/T'UNG-KU

CH'IN-CHOU SUITE

1

North of Ch'in-chou, a monastery inhabits
Wei Hsiao's ruined palace now: ancient
Mountain gate all lichen and moss, eloquent
Halls painted cinnabar and blue empty.

Moonlit dew flares on falling leaves.
Clouds chase wind over a stream. Beyond
Indifference, the clear Wei just flows
Away east in this time of grief—alone.

2

Through these borderlands, as night falls
Across rivers, drums and horns rehearse
War. Their cries rise from autumnal earth
Everywhere, wind scattering them into clouds

Grieving. Leaf-hidden, cold cicadas turn mute.
Slowly, toward the mountains, a lone bird
Returns. All ten thousand places throughout
Alike—how could I reach my journey's end?

3

Through mist stretching away to K'un-lun
Peaks, frontier rains fall in torrents.
A Ch'iang boy gazes into the Wei. Wu's envoy
Nears the Yellow River's source. As smoke

Rises over camped armies, cattle and sheep
Graze outside a summit village. Here,
Where I live, autumn grasses have grown
Calm when I close my little bramble gate.

4

Frontier shadows become autumn nights easily,
And daybreak passes imperceptibly. Rain
Tumbling from eaves down curtains, mountain
Clouds drift low across our wall. A cormorant

Gazes into a shallow well. Earthworms climb
Deep into our dry rooms. Horses, carts—
They pass desolate and alone. At my gate
Here, the hundred grasses have grown tall.

MOONLIT NIGHT THINKING OF MY BROTHERS

Warning drums have ended all travel.
A lone goose cries across autumn
Borderlands. White Dew begins tonight,
This bright moon bright there, over

My old village. My scattered brothers—
And no home to ask *Are they alive or dead?*
Letters never arrive. War comes
And goes—then comes like this again.

AT SKY'S-END THINKING OF LI PO

In these last outskirts of sky, cold
Winds rise. What are you thinking?
Will geese ever arrive, now autumn
Waters swamp rivers and lakes there?

Art resents life fulfilled, and goblins
Dine on mountain travelers with glee:
Why not sink poems to that ill-used
Ghost in the Mi-lo, talk things over?

STAYING THE NIGHT WITH ABBOT TS'AN

What drove you here, master? Cold
Autumn winds already howl. Deep, rain-
Sogged chrysanthemums litter the garden,
And in the pond, frost topples lotuses.

But the zazen emptiness you've become
Remains empty in exile. And tonight, we
Two together again, it is for us alone
This Ch'in-chou moon has risen full.

RAIN CLEARS

At the edge of heaven, tatters of autumn
Cloud. After ten thousand miles of clear
Lovely morning, the west wind arrives. Here,
Long rains haven't slowed farmers. Frontier

Willows air thin kingfisher colors, and
Red fruit flecks mountain pears. As a flute's
Mongol song drifts from a tower, one
Goose climbs clear through vacant skies.

EYEFUL

The whole district through—ripened grapes,
Autumn hills lavish with clover. Clouds
Shroud the passes, and steady frontier
Rains still haven't filled the rivers here.

Ch'iang women in their burlesque of beacon
Fires, Mongols leading camels about—
Enough. In life's twilit years, eyes broken, all
Loss and ruin—of what comes to pass, enough.

THOUGHTS COME

My sad eyes find frost and wild, blooming
Chrysanthemums on a cold wall. Broken willows
Sway in heaven's wind. And when a clear flute
Sings, my traveler's tears fall. A tower's

Shadow stretching across poised water, peaks
Gather darkness. A frontier sun stalls—then
Night. After returning birds arrive, come
Slaughter-filled cries: crows settling-in.

THE NEW MOON

Slice of ascending light, arc tipped
Aside its bellied darkness—the new moon
Appears and, scarcely risen beyond ancient
Frontiers, edges behind clouds. Silver,

Changeless—Heaven's River spreads across
Empty peaks scoured with cold. White
Dew dusts the courtyard, chrysanthemum
Blossoms clotting there with swollen dark.

POUNDING CLOTHES

Borderlands return no one. Autumn comes,
Season of fulling-stones. Soon, bitter
Cold months will sharpen separation's
Long ache. Tired, but with all my

Woman's strength, hurrying to send them
Deep into Great Wall country, I pound
Clothes here in the courtyard. And you,
My love, listen to sounds beyond the sky.

STANDING ALONE

Empty skies. And beyond, one hawk.
Between river banks, two white gulls
Drift and flutter. Fit for an easy kill,
To and fro, they follow contentment.

Dew shrouds grasses. Spiderwebs are still
Not gathered in. The purpose driving
Heaven become human now, I stand where
Uncounted sorrows begin beginning alone.

LANDSCAPE

Clear autumn opens endlessly away.
Early shadows deepening, distant
Waters empty into flawless sky.
A lone city lies lost in fog. Few

Enough leaves, and wind scattering
More, the sun sets over remote peaks.
A lone crane returning. . . . Why so late?
Crows already glut woods with night.

AN EMPTY PURSE

Though bitter, juniper berries are food
For immortals, and cirrus flushed with morning
Light. But people are common things,
These tangles of trouble my only life:

A frozen well each morning and no stove,
Cold nights without quilts. . . . In fear
Of shame an empty purse brings, I hold
In mine this one coin I keep, peering in.

SEVEN SONGS AT T'UNG-KU

1

A wanderer—O, all year, Tzu-mei a wanderer,
white hair a shoulder-length confusion, gathering

acorns all year, like Tsu the monkey sage. Under cold
skies, the sun sets in this mountain valley. No word

arrives from the central plain, and for failing
skin and bone, ice-parched hands and feet, no return, no

return there Song, my first song
                sung, O song already sad enough,
winds come from the furthest sky grieving for me.

2

Sturdy hoe, O long sturdy hoe, my white-handled
fortune—now I depend on you, on you alone

for life, there isn't a wild yam shoot to dig. Snow
fills the mountains. I tug at a coat never covering

my shins. And when we return this time, empty-handed
again—my children's tears are deafening, the four walls

harbor quiet Song, my second song
                sung, O song beginning to carry,
this village is peopled with faces grieving for me.

3

Brothers of mine, my brothers in far-off places, O
three frail brothers—is anyone strong now these

scattering lives we wander never meet? Now Mongol dust
smothers the sky, this road between us goes on forever.

Cranes flock eastward, following geese. But cranes—
how could cranes carry me there, to another life beside

my brothers Song, my third song
                    sung, O song sung three times over,
if they return, where will they come to gather my bones?

4

Sister of mine, my sister in Chung-li—devoted husband
dead young, orphan children unhinged, O my sister,

the long Huai is all deep swells, all flood-dragon fury—
how will you ever come now? Ten years apart—how will I

ever find you in my little boat? Arrows fill my eyes,
and the south, riddled with war banners and flags, harbors

another dark Song, my fourth song
                    sung, O song rehearsed four times through,
gibbons haunt the midday forest light wailing for me.

5

Mountains, all mountains and wind, headlong streams and
rain—O, the cold rain falling into withered trees falls.

And clouds never clear. Among brown weeds and ancient
city walls—white foxes prowl, brown foxes stand fast.

This life of mine—how can I live this life out in some
starveling valley? I wake and sit in the night, ten thousand

worries gathering Song, my fifth song
           sung, O song long enough now
singing my soul back, my lost soul gone to my lost home.

6

A dragon—O, a dragon in southern mountains, cragged
trees mingling their ancient branches above its pool—

when yellowed leaves fall, it sinks into hibernation,
and from the east, adders and cobras come roaming the water.

A traveler full of fear, how could I confront them?
My sword is hardly drawn before I put it away, before I

rest here Song, my sixth song
           sung, O song wearing your thoughts thin,
streams and valleys are graced by spring again for me,

7

           a man
every distinction has eluded, a man grown old only
to wander three hungry years away on mountain roads.

In Ch'ang-an, statesmen are young. Honor, wealth—
men devote themselves early. Wise men I knew long ago

live here in the mountains now. Our talk is all old
times gone by, nothing more—old friends harboring

wounded memories Song, my seventh song
           sung, O uneasy silence ending my tune,
a white sun fills the majestic sky with headlong flight.

CH'ENG-TU

ASKING WEI PAN TO FIND PINE STARTS

Standing alone, austere, they are not willows. Green—
How could such abiding green be candleberry? I imagine

Old age nurtured a thousand years in shade, and you
Finding pine starts, sturdy ones with frosty roots.

FOUR QUATRAINS

1

Bamboo shoots tall on the west, I use another gate:
Peppers in rows north of the ditch, the village behind.

When they ripen, old Chu and I will dine on plums.
When the pines tower, I'll write to Yüan about them.

2

I've planned a pier, but the water is cloud-hidden
And startled May rain sounds ice-cold. Dragons

Settled this clear stream first. Even sturdy as mountains,
What peace could bamboo on stone pilings ever bring?

3

Two yellow orioles sing from a willow. Egrets climb into
Blue sky: one trail of white. Thousand-autumn

Snows on western peaks fill my window. And at my gate,
Eastern boats anchor—ten-thousand-mile boats from Wu.

4

Some still sparse green, some lush—my rain-soaked
Herbs freshen both pavilion and porch with color.

These waste mountains are full of them—but which is
What? And roots growing into frightening shapes?

THE PLUM RAINS

Here in the Southern Capital, May plums,
Ripe and yellow, line Hsi Creek Road.
Deep and clear, the long stream flows
Away. Fine rains arrive, dark and steady,

Soaking easily through loose thatch.
Their heavy clouds will not scatter soon.
All day long, dragons delight—eddies
Curling into the bank start back out.

A GUEST

I've had asthma now for years. But here
Beside this river, our *ch'i*-sited
Home is new. Even simple noise scarce,
Its healing joy and ease are uncluttered.

When someone visits our thatch house, I
Call the kids to straighten my farmer's cap,
And from the sparse garden, gather young
Vegetables—a small handful of friendship.

THE RIVER VILLAGE

In one curve, cradling our village, the clear river
Flows past. On long summer days, the business of solitude

Fills this river village. Swallows in the rafters
Come and go carelessly. On the water, gulls nestle

Tenderly together. My wife draws a paper *go* board,
And tapping at needles, the kids contrive fishhooks.

Often sick, I need drugs and herbs—but what more,
Come to all this, what more could a simple man ask?

A FARMER

Here, beyond the smoke and dust, our
River village has eight or nine homes.
Lotus leaves float, tiny and round,
And delicate wheat blossoms feather away.

I'll grow old in this *ch'i*-sited house,
A farmer distant from the chafe of events.
Where has all my shame before Ko-hung gone,
Never asking how cinnabar is found here?

THE FARMHOUSE

Beside a clear curving river, our farmhouse
Gate opens onto an old road. The village
Market is grown over. I've gotten lazy
In this simple place, dress however I please.

Willow branches all sway easily. And loquats,
Tree after tree, scent the air. Drying
Cocked wings alight with the glare of
Late sun, cormorants crowd our fishing pier.

BOATING

Still a wanderer farming at the Southern Capital,
Spirit-wounded, I can't stop gazing north out windows.

But today, I take my wife out in the skiff. Drifting,
We watch our kids bathe in the bright, clear river.

Butterflies tumble through air, one chasing another.
Sharing stems, lotus blossoms float in natural pairs.

Tea, sugar-cane juice—we bring along what simple
Things we have, our clay jars no less now than jade.

A MADMAN

West of Wan-li Bridge, beside our grass cottage,
Po-hua Stream would delight the angler of Ts'ang-lang.

Caressed by wind, bamboo sways—elegant, flawless.
In rain, red lotus blossoms grow more and more fragrant.

Old friends with fat salaries have stopped writing,
And the kids, forever hungry, wear faces of cold despair.

About to fill some gutter, he is carefree, the madman
Grown old laughing at his growing steadily madder.

OUR SOUTHERN NEIGHBOR

Taro and chestnut remain. Our master of Chin-li,
Still less than destitute, sports a crow-peaked cap.

Well-versed hosts, your boys entertain merrily—
Even young birds, dining on the steps, feel at home.

The autumn river is four or five feet deep now,
And happily, skiffs here seat two or three. White sand,

Bamboo the color of kingfishers—in the village dusk,
We part, moonlight touching my brushwood gate anew.

BALLAD OF A HUNDRED WORRIES

Still a child's heart at fifteen. . . . I remember
running back and forth, sturdy as a brown calf.

And in September, courtyard dates and pears ripe,
I could scramble up a thousand trees in a day.

How suddenly it all passed. Already fifty, I rarely
walk, or even get up. If not asleep, I sit resting.

Today, forcing small talk and laughter for a host,
I grieve over the hundred worries crowding my life.

And when I return, the house bare as ever, my poor
wife mirrors the look she knows too well on my face.

Silly kids, still ignorant of courtesies due a father—
crying at the kitchen door, angry, they demand food.

THROUGH CENSOR TS'UI
I SEND A QUATRAIN TO KAO SHIH

Half my hundred-year life gone—another
Autumn arrives. Hunger and cold return.
Ask the Prefect of P'eng-chou how long,
In such distress, one must await rescue.

MORNING RAIN

Sounding cold dawn skies, steady winds
Tatter visions of cloud over the river.
Ducks take refuge along the island. Among
Thickets, swallows find shelter from rain.

Huang and Ch'i both refused an emperor,
Ch'ao and Yu an empire. A cup of wine,
A thatched home—that I am here as today's
Flawless morning passes gathers me in joy.

A GUEST ARRIVES

South of our home, and north, nothing but spring
Water everywhere, and gulls arriving day after day.

The path all blossoms I haven't swept for guests,
Today, for you, I open my simple gate this first time.

Dinners so far from market are nothing special,
And wine in our poor home is old and unstrained,

But if you'll drink with the old-timer next door,
I'll call over the fence, invite him for what's left.

ALONE, LOOKING FOR BLOSSOMS ALONG THE RIVER

1

The sorrow of riverside blossoms inexplicable,
And nowhere to complain—I've gone half crazy.

I look up our southern neighbor. But my friend in wine
Gone ten days drinking, I find only an empty bed.

2

A thick frenzy of blossoms shrouding the riverside,
I stroll, listing dangerously, in full fear of spring.

Poems, wine—even this profusely driven, I endure.
Arrangements for this old, white-haired man can wait.

3

A deep river, two or three houses in bamboo quiet,
And such goings-on: red blossoms glaring with white!

Among spring's vociferous glories, I too have my place:
With a lovely wine, bidding life's affairs *bon voyage*.

4

Looking east to Shao, its smoke filled with blossoms,
I admire that stately Po-hua wineshop even more.

To empty golden wine cups, calling such beautiful
Dancing girls to embroidered mats—who could bear it?

5

East of the river, before Abbot Huang's grave,
Spring is a frail splendor among gentle breezes.

In this crush of peach blossoms opening ownerless,
Shall I treasure light reds, or treasure them dark?

6

At Madame Huang's house, blossoms fill the paths:
Thousands, tens of thousands haul the branches down.

And butterflies linger playfully—an unbroken
Dance floating to songs orioles sing at their ease.

7

I don't so love blossoms I want to die. I'm afraid,
Once they are gone, of old age still more impetuous.

And they scatter gladly, by the branchful. Let's talk
Things over, little buds—open delicately, sparingly.

SPRING NIGHT, DELIGHTED BY RAIN

Lovely rains, knowing their season,
Always appear in spring. Entering night
Secretly on the wind, they silently
Bless things with such delicate abundance.

Clouds fill country lanes with darkness,
The one light a riverboat lamp. Then
Dawn's view opens: all bathed reds, our
Blossom-laden City of Brocade Officers.

TWO IMPROMPTUS

1

Under the bright, limitless, country-air
Sun, spring's water flows clear and steady.
Rushes stand everywhere along the bank,
And village paths trail from house to house.

Here, ever true to carefree ways, I follow
The master of cap-strained wine. Clear
To the end of sight, nothing bad—even
Sick many times over, my body is light.

2

Already mid-spring on the riverside,
Sunrise opens beneath blossoms again.
Hoping to see the bird, I look up. And
Turning away, I answer . . . no one there.

I read, skipping over hard parts easily,
Pour wine from full jars. . . . The old
Sage on O-mei is a new friend. He knows
It is here, in idleness, I become real.

NINE IMPROVISATIONS

1

Seeing all this wanderer's sorrow, I cannot wake from
Sorrow: spring's shameless colors crowd my pavilion.

Blossoms scattering so deep and reckless might at least
Teach these rhapsodic orioles they are trying too hard.

2

The peach and plum I planted aren't ownerless.
A hermit's wall is low, but still home. So like spring

Wind, never letting things alone: last night
It came tearing blossoms down by the branchful.

3

Knowing well how low and small my thatched study is,
River swallows come often. Their beaks clutching

Mud, they spatter my *koto* and books, and with these
Insects all-a-twitter, fly at whoever may be here.

4

March's moon broken, April arrives. I grow old
Slowly, but how many springs can I have left now?

What is inexhaustible is beyond me. I leave it there,
Just empty this cup of life's lingering limits.

5

Heartbreaking—a river spring ending. I stroll,
Cane and all, stopping along the fragrant bank.

Recklessly courting wind, willow catkins dance as
Flighty peach blossoms chase after the river current.

6

I never leave our village. Indolent, undeserving,
I call my son to close the gate, content. In these woods:

Thick wine, green moss, silence. Spring wind crosses
Jade-pure water. And out beyond, darkness falls.

7

Strewn poplar catkins carpet paths in white, and
Strung like green coins, lotus leaves dot the stream.

Pheasant chicks keep among bamboo roots, unseen.
On the sand, ducklings doze close beside mother.

8

West of the house, ready to pick, soft mulberry leaves.
Along the river path, wheat fine and delicate again. . . .

How many times can spring turn to summer in one life?
Never leave them—wine lees fragrant and sweet as honey.

9

The willow sways outside my door—delicate,
Graceful as a girl's waist at fifteen. Who was it

Saying *just another morning, same as ever?* The wild
Wind has torn hard at it, broken its longest branch.

FOUR RHYMES AT FENG-CHI POST-STATION: A SECOND FAREWELL TO YEN WU

Ending our long farewell, separation begins
Here: a second grief, empty in mountains
So green. When will we stroll, drinking wine
Together again beneath last night's moon?

Whole provinces in song for love of you,
Three reigns radiant with your talent—
I return to a river village, alone,
To nurture my crumbling years in silence.

WAYHOUSE

Outside this autumn window: dawn colors
And, high in leafless trees, wind again.
The sun appears beyond cold mountains;
A river flows through last night's mist. . . .

The enlightened reign abandons nothing.
Feeble and sick, already an old man—
Of life's consuming ruins, how much for this
Wreckage of blown tumbleweed remains?

9/9, ON TZU-CHOU CITY WALL

This night of yellow-blossom wine
Finds me old, my hair white. Joys
I ponder lost to youth, I look out
Across distances. Seasons run together.

Brothers and sisters inhabit desolate
Songs. Heaven and Earth fill drunken eyes.
Warriors and spears, frontier passes. . . .
All day, thoughts have gone on and on.

LEANING ON A CANE

Even in the city, come leaning on a cane,
I gaze at stream-side blossoms. Here,
Mountain markets close early, and riverboats
Gather at the bridge in spring. Lighthearted

Gulls flutter among white waves. Returning
Geese delight in blue skies. All things shade
Together in earth's passion. But I, all
Disparate chill, I brood over years gone by.

FAREWELL AT FANG KUAN'S GRAVE

Traveling again in some distant place, I
Pause here to offer your lonely grave
Farewell. By now, tears haven't left dry
Earth anywhere. Clouds drift low in empty

Sky, broken. Hsieh An's old *go* partner,
Sword in hand, I come in search of Hsü,
But find only forest blossoms falling and
Oriole songs sending a passerby on his way.

OUTSIDE THE CITY

It is bitter cold, and late, and falling
Dew muffles my gaze into bottomless skies.
Smoke trails out over distant salt mines
Where snow-covered peaks cast shadows east.

Armies haunt my homeland still. And war
Drums throb in this distant place. A guest
Overnight in a river city, together with
Shrieking crows, my old friends, I return.

ADRIFT

As I row upstream past a tower, the boat
glides into its shadow. Even this far
west, the stately pines of Ch'eng-tu's
widespread villages continue. And beyond,

out there in untouched country, autumn
colors heighten cold clarity. Mountain
snows bleached in its glare, sunlight
conjures exquisite rainbows among clouds.

Kids play along both banks. And though
nets and arrows are put away, the day's take
taken, wherever lotus and chestnut remains
lie scattered, the roadside bustle goes on.

The fish are all scaled, but lotus-root
covered with mud sits unwashed. Nothing
changes with us. Craving delicate beauty,
we avoid the thick squalor of things.

Over my village: scattered clouds, lovely
twilight. Here, roosting hens settle in.
Each departure like any other, where is
my life going in these isolate outlands?

Fresh moonlight falls across my clothes. It
ascends ancient walls dusted with frost.
Thick wine ready to drink since time began,
war drums break loose east in the city.

OVERNIGHT AT HEADQUARTERS

Clear autumn. Beside the well, cold *wu* trees. I pass
Night in the river city, alone, candles guttering low.

Grieving in the endless dark, horns call to themselves.
The moon drifts—no one to see its exquisite color.

Wind and dust, one calamity after another. And frontier
Passes all desolation and impossible roads, no news

Arrives. After ten desperate, headlong years, driven
Perch to perch, I cling to what peace one twig holds.

RESTLESS NIGHT

As bamboo chill drifts into the bedroom,
Moonlight fills every corner of our
Garden. Heavy dew beads and trickles.
Stars suddenly there, sparse, next aren't.

Fireflies in dark flight flash. Waking
Waterbirds begin calling, one to another.
All things caught between shield and sword,
All grief empty, the clear night passes.

SIX QUATRAINS

1

From the water east of our fence, sun
Ascends. North of home: mud-born clouds.
A kingfisher cries from bamboo heights,
And on the sand below, magpies dance.

2

Blossoms scatter, bees and butterflies
Stitching the lavish confusion with flight.
Perched in solitude, I plumb idleness—
What would guests come looking for?

3

For a new well—wellrope of braided palm
Leaves, drains cut through bamboo roots. Antic
Little boats are just tangled rigging; here,
Small paths weave our village into itself.

4

Streams swollen after headlong rains, late
Light caresses a tree's waist. Two yellow
Birds keep hidden in their nest. Where
Shattered reeds float, a white fish leaps.

5

Bamboo needles our fence. Cane is toppled
In under eaves. The land turning to sunlit
Silk slowly, reeds and the river gone
White weave together in tracery shadows.

6

Moonlight across stone, the river flows.
At the brook's mirage, clouds touch blossoms.
A perched bird knows the ancient Tao. Sails
Only drift toward night spent in whose home?

K'UEI-CHOU

CH'U SOUTHLANDS

Odd how spring in these Ch'u southlands
Arrives. The break between warm and cold
Comes early: nameless grasses on the river,
Whimsical clouds drifting among mountain peaks.

By the first month, bees are everywhere,
And birds singing much too early. It's this
Cane keeps me from leaping onto a horse
Right now, not separation from my own kind.

IMPROMPTU

A river moon cast only feet away, storm-lanterns
Alight late in the second watch. . . . Serene

Flock of fists on sand—egrets asleep when
A fish leaps in the boat's wake, shivering, cry.

K'UEI-CHOU'S HIGHEST TOWER

Above the wall's corner walkways, pennants and flags
Grieving, I stand on a soaring, mist and haze tower, alone.

In deep, fog-filled gorges, dragons and tigers sleep.
Turtles and crocodiles roam the clear, sunlit river.

The Great Mulberry spreads west to these hewn cliffs,
And Jo River shadows follow this current east. Whose child

Propped on a goosefoot cane lamenting this world? I turn
Away, white-haired descendant of nothing mourning parents.

BALLAD OF THE FIREWOOD HAULERS

K'uei-chou women, hair turned half-white, forty years
old, or fifty, and still sold into no husband's home:

no market for brides in this relentless ruin of war,
they live one long lament, nothing but grief to embrace.

Here, a tradition of seated men keeps women on their feet:
men sit inside doors and gates, women bustle in and out.

When they return, nine in ten carry firewood—firewood
they sell to keep the family going. Old as they are, they

still wear shoulder-length hair in twin virgin-knots,
matching hairpins of silver holding mountain leaves and

wildflowers. If not struggling precariously up to market,
they ravage themselves working salt mines for pennies.

Make-up and jewelry a shambles of sobs and tears (indecent
little place), clothes cold, besieged at the foot of cliffs—

if, as people say, these Wu Mountain women are such
frightful things, how could Chao-chün's village be so near?

8-PART BATTLE FORMATION

His distinction crowned the warring Three Kingdoms,
Its monument this 8-Part Battle Formation:
The river flowing through dead-still stones
Indifferent to remorse at failing to swallow Wu.

BALLAD OF THE ANCIENT CYPRESS

An ancient cypress stands before Chu-ko Liang's temple,
branches like bronze, roots like stone. Forty feet

around, bark frost-covered and flooded with rain,
it blends darkness into sky for two thousand feet.

Because king and minister met destiny together,
people still cherish this tree. When clouds come,

sending vapor the length of Wu Gorge, and the rising
moon casts a white chill across the Snow Mountains,

I think of a road winding east from my Brocade Pavilion
to that secluded temple Chu-ko Liang and his king share:

cragged trunk and branch also tower there, over ancient
plains, over empty doors and windows, dim paintings. . . .

Though its gnarled roots have spread far and deep,
to stand so distant and alone, so high in violent winds,

divine powers must nurture it. Such undeviating strength—
its source must be Creation. If a great, crumbling hall

needed roof-beams, even ten-thousand oxen would gaze
helplessly at such mountainous weight. Not yet revealed

by any craftsman's art, it already awes the world.
It doesn't resist being cut, but who could cart it away?

Though its bitter heart hasn't escaped gutting by ants,
its fragrant leaves still harbor roosting phoenixes.

No need for sullen laments—O aspirant and recluse
alike, a great nature has always been hardest to employ.

SKIES CLEAR AT DUSK

Dusk's failing flare breaks out. Clouds
Thin and drift—none return. Distant,
Bright, a rainbow drinks at the river.
Rain in the gorge falls—remnants scatter.

As ducks and cranes set out high overhead,
Fattened brown bears rest content. Autumn
Equinox. Still a wanderer, still here.
Dew on bamboo. Twilight gone spare, spare.

K'UEI-CHOU

Above K'uei-chou's wall, a cloud-form village. Below:
Wind-tossed sheets of falling rain, a swollen river

Thrashing in the gorge. Thunder and lightning battle.
Kingfisher-gray trees and ashen ivy shroud sun and moon.

War horses can't compare to those back in quiet pastures.
But of a thousand homes, a bare hundred remain. *Ai*—

Ai—the widow beaten by life's toll, grief-torn,
Sobbing in what village where on the autumn plain?

OVERNIGHT AT THE RIVERSIDE TOWER

Evening colors linger on mountain paths.
Out beyond this study perched over River Gate,
At the cliff's edge, frail clouds stay
All night. Among waves, a lone, shuddering

Moon. As cranes trail off in flight, silent,
Wolves snarl over their kill. I brood on
Our wars, sleepless here and, to right
A relentless Heaven and Earth, powerless.

NIGHT

Clear autumn: dew settles under towering skies, and among
Empty peaks, isolate nights startle my homeless spirit

Away. A distant sail stays the night: one lantern lit.
The new moon lingers. A fulling-stick cracks *once, twice.*

Bedridden, I meet southern chrysanthemums again. And geese
Heartless, letters from the north never come. Propped

On this cane, I pace the veranda: Cowherd. Northern Dipper.
Silver River spreading away—it must reach the phoenix city.

BRIDAL CHAMBER

Waist-jewels in the bridal chamber ice-cold,
Autumn winds scour jade halls. A new moon
Rises over Ch'ang-an, but the ancient
Palace still founders in Dragon Lake,

And boats moored there are distant tonight.
The clepsydra's lucid drop hasn't changed:
Ten-thousand miles north of yellow mountains,
In a white lake of dew, stand imperial tombs.

FULL MOON

Above the tower—a lone, twice-sized moon.
On the cold river passing night-filled homes,
It scatters restless gold across waves.
On mats, it shines richer than silken gauze.

Empty peaks, silence: among sparse stars,
Not yet flawed, it drifts. Pine and cinnamon
Spreading in my old garden. . . . All light,
All ten thousand miles at once in its light!

MIDNIGHT

A thousand feet up, along sheer silk
Windows, I pace West Tower. Falling stars
Flare on the river. A setting moon's
Clarity wavers on sand. Solitary

Birds are known by the woods they choose,
Great fish by their hermit deeps. Here,
Heaven and earth full of those I love,
Shield and sword make even a letter rare.

REFLECTIONS IN AUTUMN

1

Jade-pure dew wilts and wounds maple forests, deep
Wu Mountain forests rising wind-scoured from Wu Gorge.

The river's billows and waves breach sky churning, as
Clouds drifting over passes touch darkness to earth.

Thick chrysanthemums have opened tears here twice—my
Lost lives, my lone boat moored to a homesick heart. . . .

Everywhere, urgently, winter clothes are cut to pattern.
Above K'uei-chou, fulling-stone rhythms tighten at twilight.

2

Each night, slant light of dusk leaving K'uei-chou, lone city,
I find the Northern Dipper and face our bright capital.

It is true of a gibbon's voice: *after three cries, tears.*
Appointed to a stray journey on another September raft,

I lie sick, far from incense and ministerial portraits.
Among mountain towers and white-washed battlements, a flute

Mourns. There! Look there: the moon on ivy-covered cliffs—
Already, along the island, in blossoms atop reeds it flares!

3

Over a mountain city's thousand homes, I pass peaceful
Bright morning after morning in a river tower facing peaks blue

Haze thins. After two nights out, fishermen drifting home
Drift. In clear autumn, swallows persist in reckless flight.

Admonitions offered by K'uang Heng earn scant honors
Now; expounding classics is far from Liu Hsiang's heart. . . .

Wealth eluded few of my classmates—clothes and horses
All to themselves, out light and sleek at Five Tombs.

4

People call Ch'ang-an a chessboard now. And grief
Remains, after a century of consequential clamor,

Unconquered. Fresh lords move into the palaces, new
Scholars and soldiers in caps and robes replace old,

And still, gongs and drums bang in frontier passes
Due north. Armies trundle west. Feathered messages fly.

Dragons and fish withdrawn, the autumn river cold,
A peaceful, long-ago country keeps at my thoughts.

5

Palace gates at P'eng-lai face South Mountain. Gold
Stalks stand gathering dew in the Celestial River.

Hsi Wang Mu descends over Jasper Lake in the west, purple
Mist from the east filling Han-ku Pass. Palace screens

Open, pheasant-tail plumage clearing clouds away from
Sun-wreathed dragon scales: His Majesty appears and. . . .

One sleep, startled by year's end on this vast river. How many
Dawns was I at court, the blue gates all sculpted sunlight?

6

From Ch'ü-t'ang Gorge to Meandering River, ten thousand
Miles of smoke-scored wind piece this bleached autumn

Together. Through Calyx Tower arcade, frontier grief
Haunting Hibiscus Park, the imperial presence passes.

Ornate pillars and pearl screens collect yellow cranes,
And gulls scatter at brocade rigging and ivory masts. . . .

Turn toward it, land of song and dance, pity ancient
Ch'in serving kings and princes from the beginning.

7

K'un-ming, masterwork of the Han: the lake waters,
Emperor Wu's banners and flags, all within sight. And facing

Weaving Maid, moonlit emptiness woven in her loom:
The stone whale of autumn wind, its plate scales chafing.

Zizania seeds wave-tossed in pitch-dark clouds drown,
Frost sends rouge sifting off lotus seed-pods. . . . Frontier

Passes birds alone cross verge into sky. Adrift, swollen
Rivers and lakes truing up horizons—one old fisherman.

8

Where K'un-wu Road meanders with Yü-su Stream,
Tzu-ko Peak casts shadows deep into Mei-p'i Lake.

Fragrant field-rice parrot grains remains pecked-at;
Jade-green *wu* trees perch branches phoenix aging. Soon,

Exquisite women gathering kingfisher gifts for spring,
Immortals set out again in their boats. It is late.

My florid brush once defied the shape of things. I watch
Now, nothing more—hair white, a grief-sung gaze sinking.

DAWN AT WEST TOWER, FOR YÜAN

In the city, night's five brief watches
End. The tower high, rain and snow thin,
Bare hints through silk curtains promise
Clear skies. Far-off, Jade String sets.

Sunrise startles magpies from the gate,
And crows perched among rigging scatter.
But the cold river flows, an immaculate
Patience against those who will return.

NIGHT AT THE TOWER

Yin and *yang* cut brief autumn days short. Frost and snow
Clear, leaving a cold night open at the edge of heaven.

Marking the fifth watch, grieving drums and horns erupt as
A river of stars, shadows trembling, drifts in Three Gorges.

Pastoral weeping—war heard in how many homes? And tribal
Songs drifting from the last woodcutters and fishermen. . . .

Chu-ko Liang, Pai-ti: all brown earth in the end. And it
Opens, the story of our lives opens away . . . vacant, silent.

RIVER PLUMS

Buds breaking before winter's La Festival
Lavish the new year with countless plum
Blossoms. Though I know spring means well,
How will I manage this wanderer's grief?

Snow and trees share one original color,
And river wind is whitewater's child. Old
Garden . . . I cannot see my old garden:
Wu Mountain peaks crowd an erratic skyline.

TWO QUATRAINS

1

Lovely in late sun: mountains, a river,
Blossoms and grasses scenting spring wind.
Where mud is still soft, swallows fly.
On warm sand, ducks doze, two together.

2

Birds are whiter on jade-blue water.
Against green mountains, blossoms verge
Toward flame. I watch. Spring keeps
Passing. How long before I return home?

LATE SPRING

I lie ill here in these gorges, captive. Tung-t'ing Lake,
All Hsiao and Hsiang—one mirage of empty light now.

Relentless Ch'u skies rain all four seasons. And winds,
These ten-thousand-mile Wu Gorge winds never end.

Willows on its bank, a thatch home in their new shadows,
The pond out beyond city walls hints at red lotus blossoms.

Late spring. Ducks and egrets stand on the island's bank.
Chicks nestled in the flock flutter off, quick to return.

MORNING RAIN

A slight rain comes, bathed in dawn light.
I hear it among treetop leaves before mist
Arrives. Soon it sprinkles the soil and,
Windblown, follows clouds away. Deepened

Colors grace thatch homes for a moment.
Flocks and herds of things wild glisten
Faintly. Then the scent of musk opens across
Half a mountain—and lingers on past noon.

LATE SPRING: WRITTEN ON OUR
NEW NANG-WEST HOUSE

Still stranded, lamenting Three Gorges, I
Meet late spring again, its hundred voices
Soon to fall silent. And its countless
Blossoms—how long can they last? Haze

Thins in this empty valley. A majestic sun
Drifts battered waves. Where would war's
End ever begin? Among all this, wounded
Grief is nowhere to be found—nowhere.

FAILING FLARE

North of an ancient Ch'u emperor's palace, yellows fade.
Traces of rain drift west of K'uei-chou. Soon dusk's failing

Flare on the river plays across cliffs. Then returning
Clouds muffle trees. Mountain villages vanish. I manage

Life's ebb propped high on pillows, lungs sick. Against
Frontier wastes and a tormented age, I close my gate

Early. I can't stay long in these southlands, these
Jackal and tiger calamities . . . I, a yet unsummoned soul.

A SERVANT BOY COMES

Fresh greens grace haw and pear. Tinged
Apricot and plum have turned half yellow.
The courtyard silent—a boy comes bringing
Ripe, fragrant fruit in delicate baskets.

Replete with mountain wind, iced with wild
Dew, the flavors shine. Propped on pillows,
A guest of rivers and lakes, I linger over
Days and months themselves forever in each taste.

WATCHING FIREFLIES

In the autumnal, Wu Mountain night, fireflies meander
Auspiciously through openwork blinds, light on my clothes.

It startles me: books, *koto*, the whole room suddenly cold.
Returning out beyond eaves, they tangle thin stars recklessly,

Wind over railing, well-water adding to each another
Light, happen past blossoms: colors *here, there*, flashing.

Beside this desolate river, my hair white, I watch you
Sadly. On this day next year, will I be home? Will I not?

AFTER THREE OR FOUR YEARS WITHOUT NEWS FROM MY FIFTH YOUNGER BROTHER, FENG, WHO IS LIVING ALONE ON THE EAST COAST, I LOOK FOR SOMEONE TO CARRY THIS TO HIM

I hear your home is a mountain monastery
Now, in Yüeh-chou. Or maybe Hang-chou.
Dust and wind—war drags our separation out.
Clear autumn passes unnoticed. My shadow

Rooted here, among trees shrieking gibbons
Haunt, towering chimera buffet my soul away
At sea. Next spring, I'll search downriver
All the way east—white clouds and beyond.

THE LONE GOOSE

Never eating or drinking, the lone goose
Flies—thinking of its flock, calling out.
Who pities a flake of shadow lost beyond
Ten-thousand clouds? It stares far-off,

As if glimpses of them remained. Sorrows
Mount—it almost hears them again. . . .
Wild crows, not a thread of thought anywhere,
Squawk and shriek, fighting each other off.

THE MUSK DEER

Clear streams lost forever, you'll end
Served up in jade dainties. Little
Talent for the life of hermit immortals,
Unable even to resent fine kitchens—once

Times fall apart, anything is a trifle,
Faint voice at disaster's heart, anything.
Noblemen noble as thieves, gluttonous,
You'll get wolfed down in a royal trice.

THATCH HOUSE

Our thatch house perched where land ends,
We leave the brushwood gate always open. After
Dragons and fish settle into night waters,
The moon and stars drift above autumn peaks.

Dew gathers clarity, then thaws. High clouds
Thin away—none return. Women man wind-
Tossed boats anchored here: young, ashamed,
The river life battering their warm beauty.

CLEAR AUTUMN

Now high autumn has cleared my lungs, I can
Comb this white hair myself. Forever needing
A little more, a little less—I'm sick of drug-cakes.
The courtyard miserably unswept—I bow

To a guest, clutching my goosefoot cane. Our
Son copies my idylls on bamboo they praise.
By November, the river steady and smooth again,
A light boat will carry me anywhere I please.

8th MONTH, 17th NIGHT: FACING THE MOON

The autumn moon is still full tonight.
In a river village, a lone old wanderer
Raising the blinds, I return to moonlight.
As I struggle with a cane, it follows.

And bright enough to rouse hidden dragons,
It scatters roosting birds from trees. All
Around my thatched study, orange groves
Shine: clear dew aching with fresh light.

DAWN

The last watch has sounded in K'uei-chou.
Colors spreading above Yang-t'ai Mountain,
A cold sun clears high peaks. Clouds linger,
Nestled among mountain valleys, and deep

Yangtze banks keep sails hidden. Beneath
Clear skies: the clatter of falling leaves.
And deer at my bramble gate—so close
Here, we touch our own kind in each other.

DAY'S END

Oxen and sheep were brought back down
Long ago, and bramble gates closed. Over
Mountains and rivers, far from my old garden,
A windswept moon rises into clear night.

Springs trickle down dark cliffs, and autumn
Dew fills ridgeline grasses. My hair seems
Whiter in lamplight. The flame flickers
Good fortune over and over—and for what?

9th MONTH, 1st DAY: VISITING MENG SHIH-ERH AND HIS BROTHER MENG SHIH-SZU

I invade cold dew on a cane, thatch houses
Trailing smoke out into dawn light. Old,
Frail, dozing among scattered books my limit
Now, I rest often against roadside trees.

Autumn passes. What once drove me ends.
Nothing but your friendship could bring me
Here. Sipping thick wine with you, our small
Talk crystal clear, I forget the years lost.

REPLY TO A LETTER FROM MENG SHIH-ERH

Loss and ruin ended, at peace far from
Lo-yang hills, I ponder the question cloud-
Hidden peaks pose. I wouldn't leave this
Home deep among bramble. Yellow leaves

Tumble in north winds. Southern streams
Exact white-hair laments. Ten years
A guest of lakes and rivers—boundless,
My heart of lingering dusk grows boundless.

ON A TOWER

Skies bottomless, howling gibbons moan in gusting wind.
Birds scatter from clear shallows and white sand—birds

Return. Leaves from wind-torn trees fall boundlessly away,
And the Yangtze, one headlong crash, arrives without end.

Too long wandering autumn's ten-thousand-mile grief, enough
Illness already to fill a century and more, I climb this tower

To stand alone—temples bleached with trouble and worry,
Defeated. . . . And here I've just sworn off that blessèd wine.

AUTUMN PASTORAL

1

Pastoral autumn grows ever more unearthly.
A cold river jostles blue space. My boat
Tethered to Well Rope, aboriginal star,
I sited my house in Ch'u village wilderness.

There are workers here to pick ripe dates.
But I hoe these plots of sunflower wreckage
Myself. And dinners, the food of old men
Now, I share out mid-stream to the fish.

2

This gossamer life obeys an evident
Nature. Nothing turns away easily:
Fish are happiest in deep water, birds
At home in thick woods. Feeble, old,

I'm content sick and poor. Earth's
Pageant flares good and bad together.
Autumn wind blows. I totter about,
Never tired of North Mountain's ferns.

3

Music and rites to perfect imperfection,
Mountains and forests for long, steady
Happiness. . . . Gauze cap askew, I sun
My back against radiant bamboo books.

I gather windfallen pinecones, cut sky-
Chilled honeycomb open. In clogs,
I pause at sparse flecks of red and blue,
Bending toward their faint fragrance.

4

Autumn sand is white on the far bank, late
Light across mountains red. As waves
Recoil from the scales of something hidden,
Birds gather high in the wind to return.

Fulling-stones echo from every home. Axe
Strokes blend together. And soon, Ch'ing-nü
Arrives—frost drifting down, a quilt
Gift coming between me and Southern Palace.

5

I wasted my life on Unicorn portraits. Now,
Peopled with ducks and egrets, the year
Crumbles. Autumn has swollen the vast river.
Empty gorges become night's wealth of sound.

Paths lost among thousands of stacked stones,
Our sail lingers on—one flake of cloud.
Though well-versed in tribal speech, appointments
Advising lords are no certainty for my sons.

ASKING OF WU LANG AGAIN

Couldn't we let her filch dates from your garden?
She's a neighbor. Childless and without food,

Alone—only desperation could bring her to this.
We must be gentle, if only to ease her shame.

People from far away frighten her. She knows us
Now—a fence would be too harsh. Tax collectors

Hound her, she told me, keeping her bone poor. . . .
How quickly thoughts of war become falling tears.

GONE DEAF

Grown old as Ho Kuan Tzu, a hermit
Lamenting this world, like Lu P'i Weng,
How long before my sight also dims away?
For over a month now, deaf as dragons:

No autumn tears follow a gibbon's cry,
And no old-age grief a sparrow's chitter.
Mountain yellows fall. Startled, I call
Out to my son *Are there northern winds?*

RAIN

Roads not yet glistening, rain slight,
Broken clouds darken after thinning away.
Where they drift, purple cliffs blacken.
And beyond—white birds blaze in flight.

Sounds of cold-river rain grown familiar,
Autumn sun casts moist shadows. Below
Our brushwood gate, out to dry at the village
Mill: hulled rice, half-wet and fragrant.

FACING NIGHT

In farmlands outside a lone city, our
River village sits among headlong waters.
Deep mountains hurry brief winter light
Here. Tall trees calming bottomless wind,

Cranes glide in to misty shallows. Sharing
Our thatch roof, hens settle in. Tonight,
Lamplight scattered across *koto* and books
All night long, I can see through my death.

NIGHT

1

A crescent moon lulls in clear night.
Half-way into sleep, lampwicks char.
Deer wander, uneasy among howling peaks,
And falling leaves startle cicadas.

For a moment, I remember the east coast:
Mince treats, a boat out in falling snow. . . .
Tribal songs rifle the stars. Here,
At the edge of heaven, I inhabit my absence.

2

Flutes mourn on the city wall. Dusk:
The last birds cross our village graveyard.
And after decades of battle, their war-tax
Taken, people return in deepening night.

Trees darken against cliffs. Leaves fall.
The river of stars faintly skirting beyond
Borderlands, I gaze at a tilting Dipper,
A thin moon—and magpies finish with flight.

THOUGHTS

1

Throughout Heaven and Earth, whatever lives
contends. Each place has its own way,
but we all struggle inchmeal, one with another,
tangling ourselves ever tighter in the snare.

Without aristocracy, what would the lowly
grieve for? And without wealth, what could
poverty lack? O, neighborhoods may take turns
mourning, but all time is one lone corpse.

Here, in Wu Gorge, I have lived three unkempt
years out like a fluttering candle, blessed that
after a lifetime growing content with failure,
I've forgotten how splendor and disgrace differ.

Chosen for court or grown old in some outland,
I need the same workaday rice. But here, my
house of woven bramble east of city walls, I can
pick healing herbs in shaded mountain valleys.

Searching out roots beneath frost and snow,
I wear my heart away without thinking of lush
branches and vines. It isn't discipline—
this quiet life apart has always been my joy.

They say a sage is taut as a bowstring and
a fool is bent hookwise. Who knows which
I am? Taut hookwise, warming my old back
here in the sun, I await woodcutters and herdsmen.

2

I sit on our south porch in deep night,
moonlight incandescent on my knees. Sudden
winds capsizing the vast river of stars,
sunlight clears the rooftops. Things wild

wake in herds and flocks. Well-rested,
they set out with their own kind. And I,
too, hurry my kids along to scratch out
our living with the same selfish industry.

Passersby are rare under these cold, year-
end skies. Days and months grow short.
Obsessed with the scramble for glory, we
people have made bedlam lice of ourselves.

Before three emperors hatched civilization,
people ate their fill and were content.
Someone started knotting ropes, and now we're
mired in the glue and varnish of government.

Sui, inventor of fire, was the mastermind.
The catastrophe continued with Tung's edifying
histories. Everyone knows that if you light
candles and lamps, moths gather in swarms.

Sent beyond the eight horizons, the spirit
finds nothing above or below but isolate
emptiness. Departure and return: all
one motion, one timeless way of absence.

RETURNING LATE

After midnight, eluding tigers on the road, I return
home below dark mountains. My family asleep inside,

the Northern Dipper drifts nearby, sinking low
over the river. Venus blazes—huge in empty space.

Holding a candle in the courtyard, I call for two
torches. A gibbon in the gorge, startled, shrieks once.

Old and tired, my hair white, I dance and sing out.
Goosefoot cane, no sleep. . . . *Catch me if you can!*

LAST POEMS

THOUGHTS, TRAVELING AT NIGHT

In delicate beach-grass, a slight breeze.
The boat's mast teetering up into solitary
Night, plains open away beneath foundering stars.
A moon emerges and, the river vast, flows.

How will poems bring honor? My career
Lost to age and sickness, buffeted, adrift
On the wind—is there anything like it? All
Heaven and earth, and one lone sand-gull.

RIVERSIDE MOON AND STARS

The sudden storm leaves a clear, autumnal
Night and Jade String radiant in gold waves.
Celestial River a timeless white, clarity
Claims Yangtze shallows anew. Strung Pearls

Snaps, scattering shimmering reflections.
A mirror lofts into blank space. Of remnant
Light, the clepsydra's lingering drop,
What remains with frost seizing blossoms?

OPPOSITE A POST-STATION, THE BOAT MOONLIT BESIDE A MONASTERY

My boat mirroring a clear, bright moon
Deep in the night, I leave lanterns unlit.
A gold monastery stands beyond green maples
Here, a red post-tower beside white water.

Faint, drifting from the city, a crow's cry
Fades. Full of wild grace, egrets sleep.
Hair white, a guest of lakes and rivers,
I tie blinds open and sit alone, sleepless.

CHIANG-HAN

Traveling Chiang-han, lone savant spent
Between Heaven and Earth, I dream return.
A flake of cloud sky's distance, night
Remains timeless in the moon's solitude.

My heart grows strong still at dusk.
In autumn wind, I am nearly healed. Long ago,
Old horses were given refuge, not sent out.
The long road is not all they're good for.

FAR CORNERS OF EARTH

Chiang-han mountains looming, impassable,
A cloud drifts over this far corner of earth.
Year after year, nothing familiar, nothing
Anywhere but one further end of the road.

Here, Wang Ts'an found loss and confusion,
And Ch'ü Yüan cold grief. My heart already
Broken in quiet times—and look at me,
Each day wandering a new waste of highway.

LEAVING KUNG-AN AT DAWN

Again, in town to the north, a watchman's final
Clapper falls silent. Venus impetuous in the east,

Neighborhood roosters repeat yesterday's pastoral dirge.
How long can life's familiar sights and sounds endure?

My oar-strokes hushed, I leave for rivers and lakes,
Distances without promise. I step out the gate, look

Away—and suddenly, all trace has vanished. These
Drug-cakes shoring me up—they alone stay with me.

DEEP WINTER

Heaven's design blossoms and leafs out,
Stone roots bind rivers and streams: clouds
Mirroring glimmers of dawn shadow, each
Cold current traces its scar. Yang Chu's

Tears come easily here. Ch'ü Yüan's wandering
Soul cannot be summoned. As wind and
Billowing waves load the teetering dusk, we
Abandon oars for a night in whose home?

SONG AT YEAR'S END

The year ends thus: northern winds, white snow
shrouding Tung-t'ing Lake and all Hsiao and Hsiang.

Under cold skies, as fishermen tend frozen nets, Mo-yao
tribesmen shoot geese. Their mulberry bows go *twang*.

But Ch'u people like fish, not birds. Let the geese
keep flying south—killing them here is pointless.

Rice was expensive last year. Soldiers starved.
This year, falling prices have ravaged our farmers.

And as officials ride high, stuffed with wine and meat,
the looms in these fleeced straw huts stand empty.

I hear even children are sold now, that it's common
everywhere: love hacked and smothered to pay taxes.

Once, they jailed people for minting coins. But now,
cutting green copper with iron and lead is approved.

Engraved mud would be easier. Good and bad are surely
not the same, but they've long been blended together.

From the walls of ten-thousand kingdoms, painted
horns moan: such sad anthems, will they never stop?

ON YO-YANG TOWER

Having long heard about Tung-t'ing Lake,
At last I climb Yo-yang Tower. Wu and Ch'u
Spread away east and south. All
Heaven and Earth, day and night adrift,

Wavers. No word from those I love. Old.
Sick. Nothing but a lone boat. And
North of frontier passes—Tibetan horses. . . .
I lean on the railing, and tears come.

OVERNIGHT AT WHITE-SAND POST-STATION

Another night on the water: last light,
Woodsmoke again, and then this station. Here
Beyond the lake, against the enduring white of
Shoreline sand, fresh green reeds. Occurrence,

Ch'i's ten thousand forms of spring—among
All this, my lone raft is another Wandering Star.
Carried by waves, the moon's light limitless,
I shade deep into pellucid southern darkness.

FACING SNOW

Northern snows overrun T'an-chou. Mongol
Storm clouds leave ten thousand homes cold.
Windblown with scattering leaves, the rain-
Smeared, flakeless snow falls. Though my

Gold-embroidered purse is empty, my credit
Easily buys drink in silver jars. And with
No one to share the floating-ant wine,
At nightfall, I await the coming of crows.

A TRAVELER FROM

A traveler from southern darkness came,
leaving me a mermaid pearl. At its
center, indecipherable words lay
hidden—words I was unable to write.

I packed it away long ago, savings
against government clerks. And today,
opening wrappers to find it blood, I
have nothing left for taxes, not a tear.

SONG FOR SILKWORMS AND GRAIN

Every province and kingdom under heaven fronting on
the Great Wall, no city has avoided shield and sword.

Why can't the weapons be cast into ploughshares,
and every inch of abandoned field tilled by oxen?

Tilled by oxen,
spun by silkworms:

don't condemn heroes to weep like heavy rains, leave
men to grain, women to silk—let us go in song again.

MEETING LI KUEI-NIEN SOUTH OF THE RIVER

Often, long ago, I saw you in Prince Ch'i's house.
And at Ts'ui Chiu's, I sometimes heard you sing.

Just now, as we meet again, the season of falling
Blossoms gracing this world—how lovely it is.

ENTERING TUNG-T'ING LAKE

Ch'ing-ts'ao Lake is wrapped in serpent dens,
And White-Sand lost beyond Dragon-Back Island.
Ancient, cragged trees shelter flood-dikes
Here. Crow spirits dance, greeting these oars.

Returning, waves high and south winds strong, I
Fear sunsets. But tonight, a dazzling lake
Stretches into distant heavens—as if any moment,
On this raft of immortals, I will drift away.

THOUGHTS, SICK WITH FEVER ON A BOAT (THIRTY-SIX RHYMES OFFERED TO THOSE I LOVE SOUTH OF THE LAKE)

Spare us this harmony you made of earth. O
Huang Ti, occurrence unhinged still in your
Squawking pipes, and Shun, the heart of things
Wounded in your half-dead *koto*—what is your

Imperial wisdom to a wanderer caught here
And now? The year rifled with disease, my boat
Too long anchored off this eastern shore,
I watch Orion rise early over the glassy lake.

Ma Jung's flute sings. Helpless, I hold
My tunic open, like Wang Ts'an, looking out
Toward a cold homeland full of sadness.
The sorrowful year blackened over by cloud,

White houses vanish along the water in fog.
Over the maple shoreline, green peaks rise.
It aches. Winter's malarial fire aches,
And the drizzling rain won't stop falling.

Ghosts they welcome here with drums bring
No blessings. Crossbows kill nothing but owls.
When my spirits ebb away, I feel relieved.
And when grief comes, I let it come. I drift

Outskirts of life, both sinking and floating,
Occurrence become its perfect ruin of desertion.

BIOGRAPHY

The biographical information is drawn from William Hung's full-length biography, *Tu Fu: China's Greatest Poet*. Numbers on the left margin are page numbers for corresponding poems.

The T'ang China which Tu Fu knew until middle age must be counted among the great moments of human civilization. In 712 A.D. Hsüan-tsung began his 43-year rule of China. The frugality and devotion of his government were legendary; corruption was rare and taxation light. His able generals secured the borders against ever-threatening barbarians, and within China there was peace and prosperity. Under his enthusiastic patronage, arts and letters flourished. Indeed, his reign is considered the pinnacle of Chinese cultural achievement. By the time his later excesses and misjudgments began, he had created a society nearly ideal in all respects. And he had so endeared himself to the people that, even after his foolishness had left the country in ruins, their affection for him continued.

EARLY POEMS (737–745)

Tu Fu was born in 712, at the beginning of Hsüan-tsung's reign. Though not of the aristocracy's highest stratum, his father came from a long line of respected scholar-officials. His mother, who died shortly after his birth, was the great-granddaughter of Emperor ⊥ ai-tsung, the founder of the T'ang Dynasty. This heritage gave Tu Fu widespread and prominent connections, and in his life of poverty and lonely wandering, he would often depend upon their generosity. Although he was the only surviving child of this marriage, his father's remarriage added three step-brothers and a step-sister to the family.

Very little is known of Tu's early life. Oddly, he seems to have spent a great deal of time separated from his family. He received a classical education and, by the age of fourteen, was apparently impressing notable scholars with his talent. In his late teens, he began traveling. And when he was twenty, he traveled to southeastern China, where he stayed for four years. This extensive traveling at such a young age, and apparently not with his family, was highly unusual.

At twenty-four, in order to prepare for the imperial examinations, Tu Fu went to Ch'ang-an, the nation's very cosmopolitan capital, a city of two million inhabitants. In the capital, his talent and broad experience attracted considerable attention. His ancestral home was Tu-ling, a village ten miles south of Ch'ang-an, so he was presented as a candidate from the capital's prefecture, a position which carried considerable prestige and a virtual guarantee of success in the exams. These *chin-shih* examinations were the traditional means of securing official appointments in the capital. They consisted of poetry and prose composition, as well as the writing of essays on current political questions and the Confucian and Taoist classics.

Any young man from the educated, aristocratic class aspired passionately to serve as an official. Not only were the practical advantages considerable (intellectual/artistic opportunity and companionship, wealth, prestige), but in the Confucian order, helping the emperor care for the people was a scholar's only proper place in the universe. Consequently, it was a terrible blow when a very impressive young Tu Fu, a devoted Confucian throughout his life, somehow failed the examinations.

The following year, 737, Tu left Ch'ang-an and trav-
3 eled in the eastern countryside near Yen-chou, where his father was the assistant prefect. He spent three leisurely years there—riding, hunting, sightseeing, and socializing. His travels were brought to an end by his father's death in 740. Tu resettled the family, for which he was now responsible, in a village near Lo-yang, where the family graveyard was located. After the twenty-seven-month mourning period, Tu moved to
3 Lo-yang, the eastern capital. He remained there for several years, probably supporting himself with freelance literary work.

In 744, Tu Fu met Kao Shih and Li Po in a country wineshop east of Lo-yang and traveled with them briefly. The following year, he left Lo-yang and returned to the eastern countryside near Yen-chou,
4 though this time he lived more the life of a recluse. Tu
5 was visited here by Li Po. Li, who was eleven years older than Tu, was already quite famous, and Tu admired him inordinately. But this was to be the last time the two poets would meet. It seems Tu Fu quickly passed from Li Po's mind (only two of Li Po's surviving poems are addressed to Tu Fu, both written at the time of their parting), but Tu often thought of Li and, over the years, wrote more than a dozen poems concerning him.

CH'ANG-AN I (746–755)

Tu Fu returned to the capital at the end of 745, after an eight and one-half year absence, and began to see first-hand the results of a scarcely believable deterioration in the emperor's wisdom. The military had become unmanageably large, as had the administration, where extravagance and corruption were endemic. The taxes needed to support this government had become an unbearable burden for the people, whose relative prosperity was in dramatic decline. The emperor was intoxicated with his favorite concubine, the infamous Yang Kuei-fei, whose ostentatious and corrupt influence was pervasive. Occupying himself more and more with entertainments and the Taoist pursuit of immortality, he left the affairs of state to an equally dangerous person: Li Lin-fu, the prime minister. To consolidate his power, Li systematically eliminated anyone he could not be certain of controlling. Many of his victims were among Tu's friends in the capital. Fortunately, Tu was not a man of great importance, otherwise his association with these people would have made him subject to Li's enmity as well.

As China had long been beleaguered by encroaching barbarians, virtually everyone in the empire, including Tu Fu, applauded the early military successes on the frontiers. But the increasing military adventurism being orchestrated by Li Lin-fu had become alarming. He considered many military governors in the border regions a personal threat, so he replaced them with largely illiterate barbarian generals who were all too willing to carry out the expansionist program he convinced the emperor to pursue. Soon, the emperor controlled only the palace army directly, while foreign generals with no real loyalty to the T'ang government controlled vast autonomous armies and territories, setting what should have been an all too obvious stage for the catastrophe soon to follow.

Tu Fu's reason for returning to Ch'ang-an undoubtedly involved his tireless hope of obtaining a governmental position. In 747, after Tu had been in the capital for a year, the emperor ordered a special examination for all accomplished scholars not already in government service. But again, Tu was to be dissappointed. Li Lin-fu, who administered the exam, failed all candidates and then praised the gullible emperor for having already brought every worthy man of the empire into his service.

10–14 With the exception of some time spent as a recluse in the nearby mountains, Tu remained in Ch'ang-an for the next five years. Though he received no official recognition, he was quite well-respected and counted among his friends and patrons some of China's most eminent literary and political figures. Several of Tu's *fu* (rhyme-prose) were eventually shown to the emperor, who was so impressed that he immediately "summoned" Tu, telling him to await further word. Tu became an instant celebrity and always remembered this as one of the great events in his life. He waited

14 until the following year, 752, when the emperor ordered a special examination for him.

Tu Fu passed the examination—which was given with great fanfare and attended by many dignitaries—though not with any particular distinction. That this exam, like the one in 747, was administered by Li Lin-fu may help to explain Tu Fu's mediocre showing. Rather than being appointed an advisor to the emperor, as was his hope, Tu was put on the list of those awaiting routine civil service assignments. As Li Lin-fu had brought this appointment system to a virtual standstill, Tu knew that even a routine position might now be years away.

15 Severely disappointed, he retired to Tu-ling, his ancestral village just south of Ch'ang-an, where he had somehow acquired farmland.

The date of Tu Fu's marriage is uncertain, but his first son, Tu Tsung-wen, was born at Tu-ling. Tu Fu, whom history has revered as a devoted father and husband, now began a desperate struggle to support his wife and children. Over the next four years, Tu's wife apparently gave birth to two daughters and two more sons. One of these sons died in 755 (p. 22), however, leaving the couple with two daughters and two sons for most of their married life. In 769, another daughter was born, but she died one year later.

Li Lin-fu died in 753, one year after Tu moved to Tu-ling. Certain that the appointment system would soon be revitalized, Tu returned to the capital. By early summer, the struggling family was settled in the south-16   east part of the city, on the bank of Meandering River. Here, Tu developed chronic asthma and his lifelong battle with ill-health began.

A desperate, year-long wait in Ch'ang-an culminated not with a position in the imperial court, however, but 17–18   with sixty days of steady rain. Houses crumbled and the crops were ruined. In the attempt to provide for his family, Tu Fu first moved back to Tu-ling, and then north to Feng-hsien where he managed to find help and support them through the winter. The following year, he left his family in Feng-hsien and returned to Ch'ang-an, hoping to settle his appointment. Finally, in early winter of 755, Tu Fu was granted a position in 18–21   the palace of the crown prince, so he returned to Feng-hsien in order to move the family back to Ch'ang-an. Instead, his long-awaited success fell victim to the major political event of his time: the devastating An Lu-shan rebellion.

CH'ANG-AN II (756–759)

The T'ang Dynasty never fully recovered from An Lu-shan's rebellion and the chronic militarism which it spawned. The fall in census figures from 53 million before the fighting to only 17 million afterwards summarizes its catastrophic impact. Of 53 million people,

36 million were left either dead or displaced and homeless.

An Lu-shan, who had become the most powerful of the non-Chinese military governors on the frontier, launched his campaign from the northeast in December of 755. Although most people knew the rebellion was imminent, the self-involved emperor would hear nothing of it, so the loyal forces were unprepared to defend the country. In January, 756, the rebel armies captured Lo-yang, the eastern capital, and An declared himself emperor of a new dynasty. The imperial forces defending the capital were concentrated in T'ung-kuan Pass. When the court, in its folly, compelled the commanding general to abandon his secure defensive position and attack, the army was decimated by the rebel forces, and Ch'ang-an was left defenseless. The court escaped with the palace army, and in mid-July the capital surrendered to the rebels who sacked it as brutally as they had Lo-yang.

Having watched the foolhardy court ruin the country, the palace army was mutinous. At Ma-wei poststation, 40 miles west of Ch'ang-an, they killed the prime minister and Yang Kuei-fei, whom they recognized to be the primary corrupting influence in the court. Overcome by remorse for his incompetence and the death of his beloved concubine, Hsüan-tsung turned the throne over to the crown prince and traveled southwest to Ch'eng-tu. With the court ministers and palace army, the new emperor went north to organize the resistance, where two able generals and their sizable armies soon joined him. The rebel successes continued, and the first of many revolts by Chinese military governors in the interior began.

After the capital fell to An Lu-shan's army, Tu Fu resettled his family further north, at Fu-chou, where he hoped they would be safe from the rebels. His wife was again pregnant, but having heard that the crown prince (in whose service he now was) had become emperor, he left to join the exile court. But for unknown reasons, he next appears in Ch'ang-an where,

25–27 like all of the citizens, he was confined to the city. Although he was at times hiding from the rebels, it seems he generally moved freely around the city— perhaps because his official rank and reputation as a poet were so insignificant, perhaps because he was able to elude and/or keep his identity from the rebel authorities. In any case, he avoided being taken to serve in the rebel court at Lo-yang. Tu remained in Ch'ang-an for nearly a year. During this time, as if things weren't bad enough, he apparently contracted malaria. In spite of his boast that chanting certain of his poems could cure the disease, he was to suffer relapses for the rest of his life.

Tu Fu managed to escape from the city in May of 757 and make his way to the exile court at Feng-hsiang. When he arrived there, he was appointed Re-

28–29 minder. According to tradition, the duty of a Reminder was to advise the emperor and to point out any errors or oversights he might make. In Tu's time, however, Reminders were expected to do little more than take part in the imperial pageantry. The new emperor, Su-tsung, who was becoming suspicious and unreasonable, soon demoted Fang Kuan, one of his highest ministers. As Tu took his traditional advisory duties quite seriously (and Fang Kuan was his patron/friend), he pointed out the emperor's short-sightedness. Su-tsung immediately had Tu arrested, and only after the intervention of several other ministers was he released.

Tu had by now been separated from his family for a year and, in such calamitous times, had no idea what might have befallen them. In fact, the war had reportedly reached Fu-chou, so he suspected that the family had been killed, or at least driven away—a fear strengthened by the fact that his letters to them hadn't been answered. Finally, in September, he received a letter from his wife. Not only was the family still safe in Fu-chou, but another son (Tu Tsung-wu) had been born. With news of them, he was now anxious to return to his family, and the emperor was hardly reluctant to allow the pesky man a leave of absence from the court. After a difficult journey which took over two weeks, he arrived home at the beginning of October.

30–33

A month later, loyal forces drove the rebels from the capital. They soon recovered Lo-yang, as well, and drove the rebels into the east. Tu Fu, overjoyed by the rebels' defeat, returned to Feng-hsiang and joined in the emperor's jubilant return to the capital. In January, 758, his family joined him in Ch'ang-an, where he was happily attending court and accompanying the emperor in victory celebrations. Although a rebel army remained at large in the east, most rebel forces had either surrendered or been defeated, and the rebellion seemed to have ended. Tu was optimistic and working diligently in the position he had so long desired.

34

By spring, however, the poorly advised emperor began to banish worthy officials, notably Fang Kuan and his associates, many of whom were Tu Fu's close friends. That summer, because of his association with the Fang Kuan group, Tu Fu himself suffered a mild form of banishment. He was sent to Hua-chou, a town between Ch'ang-an and Lo-yang, where he served as Commissioner of Education.

35

The following January, apparently on official business, Tu went to Lo-yang. He used this opportunity to advise the commanders who had been sent to subdue the remaining rebels. In fact, this may well have been the real purpose of his trip. His advice was ignored, though it was quite astute, as it turned out, including specific warnings against the very dangers

35–36

that would lead to an unforeseen and disastrous defeat for the loyal forces. The most powerful rebel commander had surrendered the previous year, but in exchange for his surrender, the emperor left him in command of his army. In April, this general turned on the T'ang government and staged a surprise attack at Yeh City, which sent the massive loyal army into disarray and retreat toward the west. The loyalists were able to defend Lo-yang for another six months, but the city was clearly threatened and its people fled. Tu Fu also fled, returning to his home in Hua-chou.

36–38

Because his bureaucratic routine was unbearably tedious and his position in government a source of danger, Tu soon began to consider leaving official life and devoting himself to writing. In late August, his frustrations compounded by the intensifying rebel threat and a famine which gripped the region, he resigned his post and moved the family to Ch'in-chou, 330 miles to the west.

CH'IN-CHOU/T'UNG-KU (759)

The conflict between a deeply felt Confucian responsibility to serve the government and a desire to live the more spiritually rewarding life of a recluse has always been endemic among China's scholar-officials, and a great many of them chose retirement sooner or later. However, Tu Fu's decision was remarkable in that, unlike most other men who left official life (T'ao Yüan-ming is the legendary exception among his literary forebears), Tu had no apparent means of support. This momentous decision to free himself from the frustrations and dangers of public life for the solitude which would allow him to concentrate on his writing resulted in great hardship for him and his family, but it also produced spectacular artistic results: not only

were over 80% of his surviving poems written after
leaving Hua-chou (the last eleven years of his life),
but their depth and complexity increased dramatically.

Ch'in-chou was just what Tu had hoped to find—a
beautiful area of remote highlands on the western
frontier. Although the task of resettling was compli-
cated by continuing asthma and his third relapse of
41–47   malaria, Tu seemed generally pleased and ready to
stay there. However, several Tibetan tribes which had
only ostensibly submitted to the T'ang government
lived nearby, and they had become menacing. As Tu
seems to have sensed, this foreshadowed the Tibetan
invasion which was to begin in this province the fol-
lowing year. Feeling threatened, and having found no
means of support, the family moved south in search
of a more secure life after less than two months in
Ch'in-chou.

They next intended to settle at a village in the dis-
trict of T'ung-ku. Although the area was again quite
47–50   beautiful, they found only increasing poverty and hun-
ger there, so they left after six weeks. The family then
traveled further south, making a difficult crossing over
the perilous Ch'in Ling Mountains. This route was so
formidable, in fact, that part of the road was actually
a wooden structure suspended on the side of a large
cliff. After a journey of 500 miles, they reached the
city of Ch'eng-tu, in the Szechwan Basin, at the end of
the year.

CH'ENG-TU (760–765)

Ch'eng-tu, the capital of Western Chien-nan province
(present-day Szechwan), was the largest and most im-
portant city in western China. Its size and remoteness
attracted many refugees from the ravaged central plain.
When Tu Fu arrived, he found a number of well-placed

friends and relatives in the area, and their assistance
was so generous that he soon built a comfortable home
in a small village outside the city. This "thatch hut"
became a kind of hallowed memory for later Chinese—
there is still a memorial temple (now within Ch'eng-tu
City) on the supposed site. Though revered as the
humble farmhouse portrayed in Tu's poems, the house
was actually quite comfortable. It was located south-
west of Ch'eng-tu, on the north bank of a small river.
Tu Fu was charmed by the rusticity and simplicity of
this farm village, but he also enjoyed the advantage of
neighbors who were from the scholar-official class.

In spite of ill-health (in Ch'eng-tu, severe rheuma-
tism is added to his afflictions), the completion of his
53–56   house in the spring of 760 marked the beginning of
two peaceful and happy years. Finally, he had found
his long-desired hermitage, albeit far from his home-
land in the capital region. When the first autumn in
57–58   their new home arrived, the family's poverty was again
serious, largely because the military governor, Tu Fu's
richest patron, had been replaced by a man unknown
to Tu. This difficult period passed, however, and the
59–64   family managed well enough for another year on the
generosity of friends and the salaries from various lit-
erary commissions.

In the spring of 762, the retired Emperor Hsüan-
tsung died, and the health of Emperor Su-tsung was
very poor. Soon, a power struggle was raging in the
court and, abandoned in the midst of the fighting, the
emperor died. The crown prince emerged from the strug-
gle as the new Emperor Tai-tsung. Yen Wu, who had
recently been appointed military governor at Ch'eng-tu,
was summoned to Ch'ang-an soon afterward. Yen Wu
and Tu Fu were old and close friends (they were ban-
ished from Ch'ang-an in 758 because they were both
members of the group associated with Fang Kuan), so
Tu accompanied Yen to Mien-chou, about one hundred

65 miles northeast of Ch'eng-tu, and there bid him fare-
well.

Within days of this parting, a violent revolt broke
out in Ch'eng-tu and spread throughout the province.
Tu Fu fled about one hundred miles east to Tzu-chou.
As Yen Wu's close friend, he may have been high on
the rebels' list of enemies; on the other hand, the rebel
leader was an admiring friend of his, and he may have
wanted to avoid being implicated. In any case, his
flight was so precipitous that he was unable to take
his family with him. Tu spent several months alone
65 and unsettled in the Tzu-chou region before his family
managed to join him there. The revolt was put down in
September, but because the local military situation was
uncertain and Tibetan armies were threatening the
province, Tu seems to have been in no hurry to return
to Ch'eng-tu. Indeed, he was not to return for two
years.

These years passed uneventfully for Tu and his
66 family—never in great distress, but never settled and
content, as they had been in Ch'eng-tu. Tu Fu's prin-
ciple concern was resettling his family. He always had
plans underway, but circumstances never allowed him
to carry through with any of them. Meanwhile, he so-
cialized a good deal, did some sightseeing, and made
several extended trips to nearby cities.

Loyal forces defeated the rebels occupying Lo-yang
in November, 762, and they too sacked the city. They
continued to push eastward until, in February of 763,
the long and cataclysmic An Lu-shan rebellion came
to an end. The victory was, to a large extent, only
nominal however. Although the rebel leader (An Lu-
shan's son, who had murdered his father) was dead,
the victory was secured primarily because many rebel
commanders surrendered to the advancing loyal army.
As payment for their surrenders, these men were re-
instated in the same positions they had held in the

rebel government, retaining control over the same ter-
ritories and armies. This simply confirmed the north-
east as an autonomous region.

China had little chance to savor the illusory victory
in the east before the Tibetan threat in the west be-
came apparent. The Tibetans had been steadily en-
croaching into the northwest for several years and
were, by now, well-established only seventy-five miles
from the capital. Kao Shih, now military governor of
Western Chien-nan, attacked them from the south, but
was unsuccessful. That autumn he lost several of the
province's northern and western prefectures. And pre-
occupied with the unflagging court intrigues, the palace
failed to respond. In fact, the emperor was apparently
kept uninformed of the Tibetan threat until the last
minute. In November, he fled and the newly rebuilt
capital fell to the Tibetans who plundered it thor-
oughly. The Chinese army regrouped and recaptured
the capital two months later. However, the Tibetans
were to occupy northwestern China for another thir-
teen years. They kept the Chinese in a constant state
of fear, and their annual autumn offensives under-
mined T'ang attempts to recover from the An Lu-shan
rebellion.

Soon after returning to the capital, the emperor of-
fered Tu Fu an appointment in Ch'ang-an with an in-
crease in rank. However, as the position was nearly
identical to the one he had left in Hua-chou, and the
capital was so unstable militarily and politically, he
did not accept. In February, 764, Yen Wu was again
appointed military governor in Ch'eng-tu, and Tu
gladly returned to his thatch hut on the river. The
family was to spend another year in the village, but it
would not be so idyllic a time as their first two years
there.

In June, after considerable persuasion, Yen Wu con-
vinced Tu Fu to accept a position as his military ad-

visor. The Tibetans still held prefectures in the prov-
67–69   ince, so there was a good deal of military activity, and
Tu was kept quite busy. By autumn, the Tibetans had
been driven from the province, and Tu, hardly in good
health and never able to endure the bureaucratic rou-
69   tine, was allowed to spend most of his time at home.

Kao Shih, who had been recalled to the capital with
great honors, died the following February. Then, in
70–71   May, Yen Wu died. How it was related to Yen Wu's
death is not known, but at about the same time, Tu
and his family left Ch'eng-tu. Perhaps he anticipated
trouble, for within six months another rebellion broke
out in Ch'eng-tu and spread throughout the province.

K'UEI-CHOU (765–768)

The Tu family sailed down the Min River to the
Yangtze, then down the Yangtze to Yün-an, arriving
there in early autumn. Tu was again very ill, so the
75   family was forced to remain in Yün-an until late the
following spring (766). They then made a seventy-mile
75   journey downstream through the first of the Yangtze
Gorges to K'uei-chou City. K'uei-chou was located
among the spectacular gorges formed where the
Yangtze cut its way through the formidable Wu Moun-
tains. It sat on a cliff overlooking the river at the
mouth of the Three Gorges (Ch'ü-t'ang Gorge, Wu
Gorge, Shih-ling Gorge), a two-hundred-mile stretch
of very narrow canyons legendary for the river's vio-
lence and the towering cliffs alive with shrieking
gibbons.

Tu Fu was now on the very outskirts of the civilized
world. Although traces of Chinese civilization did reach
cities along the river, the nearly impenetrable Wu
Mountain complex was populated only by aboriginal
tribes speaking dialects largely unintelligible to Tu Fu.

In spite of, or perhaps more likely, because of this, the two years which Tu spent in the K'uei-chou area were to be his most productive period. Not only were more than one quarter of his surviving poems written there, but they open a new dimension of stark, elemental experience.

75   Tu stayed briefly in K'uei-chou City. Then, before spring ended, he moved to a rented house on the steep
76–78   farmland slopes northwest of the city, where he struggled to make ends meet. Although a summer drought frustrated his attempts at farming, he seems to have found some literary employment in the city.

One of Yen Wu's generals in Ch'eng-tu was transferred to K'uei-chou as prefect and military commander of the region. This man, who had been an acquaintance of Tu Fu's in Ch'eng-tu, became a generous patron of the displaced and struggling poet. He hired Tu as an unofficial secretary with only token responsibilities and, that autumn, arranged an apartment for him atop West Tower. In this dramatic setting over the southwest corner of the city, his family remaining at the country house and well-provided for, Tu was free enough from distractions and worry that he could con-
79–85   centrate on his writing. He remained in West Tower through winter and into the spring of 767.

In addition to his chronic asthma, Tu seems to have become diabetic and, that winter, he was again suffering from malaria. By late spring, worn down by his illnesses and no longer able to fulfill even his token responsibilities as the prefect's secretary, Tu was again longing for a quiet life in the countryside. The prefect apparently gave him a substantial parting gift, because Tu soon purchased an estate and a rice farm in the country near K'uei-chou.

The estate, located on a large stream west of K'uei-chou, included a house, guest-house, orchards, and flower gardens. The rice farm was in a small farming village east of the city. It also had a house, and offered a good view of the Yangtze. Tu divided his time between the two houses and managed his diverse farming operations. His health improved markedly. He was comfortably settled as a gentleman farmer and financially secure. But that autumn, his strength restored by this happy state of affairs, Tu was again thinking of returning to Ch'ang-an and his home in nearby Tu-ling, where he still owned a farm. The Tibetans launched another offensive in September, however, so his departure was delayed through the winter.

86
–102

LAST POEMS (768–770)

In March, 768, having learned that the Tibetans had been beaten back, Tu sailed through the spectacular Three Gorges to Chiang-ling on the central Yangtze plain, a 250-mile journey. Tu Fu's plan was to sail down the Yangtze to the Han River, then up the Han to Ch'ang-an. However, Tu stopped at Chiang-ling, perhaps because he found a number of close friends living there, and rented a house. Here, the family lived in relative comfort until mid-autumn.

105–7

When news of still another Tibetan invasion reached him, Tu seems to have abandoned his plans to return to Ch'ang-an. Instead, the family moved to nearby Kung-an, where they were supported for several months by a wealthy patron. In January of 769, the Tu family again set out down the Yangtze, arriving in Yo-chou at the end of the month. From there, they sailed south, across Tung-t'ing Lake, to the Hsiang River which enters the lake from the south. Tu must have hoped to get assistance from the governor of this province, who was a friend, but the governor died soon after Tu's arrival. After being delayed for several months by illness, Tu finally settled the family in T'an-

107–8
108–9

109

chou. Here, a baby girl was born, the family's poverty
intensified, and Tu's poor health continued. The family
110   remained in T'an-chou until the following spring.
–11   In early May, 770, a revolt broke out in T'an-chou.
The provincial governor was murdered and the city
seized. Once again, the Tu family was forced to flee.
They planned to take a boat to Ch'en-chou, 460 miles
south on the Hsiang River, where they could expect
assistance from Tu's uncle, the local prefect. But by
mid-summer, when the revolt was put down, they were
still far short of their destination. When the good news
reached them, they quickly returned to T'an-chou.

By autumn, Tu had again settled on returning to his
home at Ch'ang-an. The Tibetans launched another in-
vasion in early October. His baby girl fell ill and died
before autumn had ended. And that winter, on a boat
112   traveling north along the eastern shore of Tung-t'ing
–13   Lake, Tu Fu himself died.

NOTES

Page references are given in the running heads; numbers on the left margin refer to line numbers. In cases where a poem has several sections, line numbers are preceded by section numbers (e.g., 4.3). T stands for Title.

With the exception of passages from Burton Watson's *The Complete Work of Chuang Tzu*, all translations are my own.

EPIGRAPH

My epigraph is borrowed from a Tu Fu poem which I have not translated: "Written in Admiration After Hearing Hsü Shih-yi Chant His Poems One Night."

EARLY POEMS

GAZING AT THE SACRED PEAK

T Sacred Peak: Tu Fu has hiked part-way up T'ai Mountain. As the most revered of China's five sacred mountains, its summit was the destination of many pilgrims.

3 Creation: literally "create change" (*tsao-hua*), an ongoing process: a kind of deified principle.

4 *Yin* and *yang:* These philosophic terms also refer to northern and southern mountain slopes—the northern always being in shadow and the southern in light.

VISITING FENG-HSIEN TEMPLE AT LUNG-MEN

T Lung-men: a spectacular complex of cave temples located

six miles south of Lo-yang. Not actually a cave temple, Feng-hsien was a wooden structure built against the cliff. The colossal sculptures carved from the cliff for its shrine (including a thirty-five-foot Buddha) are one of the glories of Chinese Buddhist sculpture.

WRITTEN ON THE WALL AT CHANG'S HERMITAGE

7 *On a whim:* The recluse Wang Hui-chih (d. 388) set out "on a whim" to visit a friend. When he arrived at the friend's house, however, the mood had vanished, so he simply returned home without seeing his friend.

FOR LI PO

3 Ko Hung: Taoist alchemist and writer (283–343) famous for discovering how to produce the elixir of immortality. There were two schools of Taoism: esoteric (concerned primarily with the pursuit of longevity) and philosophic (following Lao Tzu and Chuang Tzu). Tu Fu considered the esoteric school humorous, at best, but he took the philosophic school quite seriously.

CH'ANG-AN I

A LETTER FROM MY BROTHER AT LIN-YI ARRIVES

1 Dual Principles: Heaven and Earth, *yang* and *yin* (p. 133).
10 Mu Wang: a legendary emperor (d. 946 B.C.) who used these mythical turtles and crocodiles to form a bridge.
11 Magpies . . . Celestial River: Once each year, magpies form a bridge over the Celestial River (Milky Way)— see p. 155.
21 Flood-charm: sculpted peach pits thrown into rising waters as a charm against flooding.
22 Peach branches of immortality: There was a vast peach tree on P'eng-lai, island of the (Taoist) immortals in the Eastern Sea. Anyone who tasted its fruit became immortal.

24   P'eng-lai tortoise: One myth holds that this vast sea tortoise supports P'eng-lai on its shell. In another myth, it supports the entire earth.

SONG OF THE WAR-CARTS

T   This poem is in the *yüeh-fu* ballad form, the traditional form for poems of social protest, which allows rather extreme metrical irregularities. There was no compulsory military service. However, press-gangs were used in times of heavy fighting, when there weren't enough volunteers to fill the military's needs.

14   Emperor Wu: Han emperor (156–87 B.C.). Placing ballads in the Han Dynasty was a *yüeh-fu* convention, used when the poem was likely to offend those in power.

20   Ch'in: the Ch'ang-an region, once controlled by the ancient state of Ch'in.

34   Sky-Blue Seas: Koko Nor (Chinghai Hu), a large lake on a plain in the Tibetan highlands of western China.
     Weeping of old ghosts: Until men killed in battle are buried, their spirits linger nearby weeping.

CROSSING THE BORDER

T   Another example of the *yüeh-fu* ballad. The speaker in this sequence is a young man, or perhaps several young men, drafted into military service. Originally, *yüeh-fu* were folk songs, often critical of the government, which were collected by the Han emperor Wu's Music Bureau ("*yüeh-fu*" means "Music Bureau") to gauge the sentiments of the common people. Hence, as poets adopted the form, using a common person as the poem's speaker became a convention (pp. 37, 46).

3.7 Unicorn Pavilion: where portraits of China's great heroes and statesmen hung.

5.6 Mongol: Though not an entirely satisfactory solution, "Mongol" seems to be the best rendering of "*hu*," which refers to the whelter of barbarian tribes which had lived north and west of China. For Tu Fu, "*hu*" was as much a general term of scorn as it was a proper name, so it called up the entire historic succession of these threatening tribes.

NEW YEAR'S EVE AT TU WEI'S HOME

T   Being with one's family for New Year's Eve was of great importance (Tu Wei was only a distant cousin, not part of Tu Fu's immediate family). The family stayed up all night celebrating. Every light in the house was kept burning and, to keep evil spirits out, doors and windows were sealed closed with strips of paper until just before dawn, when everyone went outside.

5   On New Year's Day, the first day of spring, all Chinese counted themselves a year older.

MEANDERING RIVER: THREE STANZAS, FIVE LINES EACH

T   Meandering River: After flowing through southeast Ch'ang-an, Meandering River entered a lake, which was part of a large park in the southeast corner of the capital. Somewhat confusingly, the stream, lake, and park were all known by the same name: Meandering River. The park served as a lavish country resort for those privileged enough to own homes along the lakefront there. In late autumn, when this poem was written, the park was abandoned and the houses were closed up for winter.

2.1   Neither modern nor ancient: The poem's title is in the same form as that used for the ancient poems in the *Shih Ching* (*Classic of Poetry*). However, the poems themselves are in the seven-character quatrain form (broken by the addition of a fifth line), a very recent invention.

3.3   South Mountain: In the *Shih Ching*, South Mountain literally refers to the mountains near Tu Fu's home. However, it also carries figurative connotations in such passages as "like the timelessness of South Mountain" (*Shih Ching*—166/6). This figurative sense becomes predominant in later writers, most notably T'ao Yüan-ming (see p. 137, e.g.).

3.4 Li Kuang: Han Dynasty military commander (d. 125 B.C.) who lived in the mountains near Tu-ling. He once encountered a fierce tiger and shot an arrow at it. But when the arrow hit its target, Li saw that the tiger was, in fact, only a stone. Li rarely spoke.

9/9, SENT TO TS'EN SHEN

T 9/9: festival celebrated on the 9th day of the 9th month. Chrysanthemum wine (believed to enhance longevity), poetry composition (often on the subject of chrysanthemums), and the contemplation of absent friends and relatives played an important part in the holiday observances. Ts'en Shen: Tu Fu's friend, still highly respected for his poetry. Like Tu Fu, he was banished in 758 because of his association with Fang Kuan.

17 Tu Fu is playing on a couplet written by T'ao Yüan-ming
–20 (T'ao Ch'ien—365–427), the great poet-recluse, whom Tu admired very much. It is from the fifth in a sequence entitled "Drinking Wine":

> Picking chrysanthemums at my eastern hedge,
> I glimpse South Mountain in the distance.

AUTUMN RAIN LAMENT

3 Ox . . . horse: borrowed from *Chuang Tzu* 42/17/1:

> The time of the autumn floods came and the hundred streams poured into the Yellow River. Its racing current swelled to such proportions that, looking from bank to bank or island to island, it was impossible to distinguish a horse from a cow. Then the Lord of the River was beside himself with joy, believing that all the beauty in the world belonged to him alone.
>
> (Watson, 175)

4 Ching . . . Wei: major rivers which converge just northeast of Ch'ang-an, then flow into the Yellow River.

4   Chi and Chieh: archetypal ministers who served Emperors Yao and Shun.

5   Hui Tzu: a hair-splitting logician and favorite target of Chuang Tzu. In *Chuang Tzu* 2/1/37 (cf. 3/1/42), Hui Tzu says to Chuang Tzu:

> The king of Wei gave me some seed of a huge gourd. I planted them, but when they grew up, the fruit was big enough to hold five piculs. I tried using it for a water container, but it was so heavy I couldn't lift it. I split it in half to make dippers, but they were so large and unwieldy that I couldn't dip them into anything. It's not that the gourds weren't fantastically big—but I decided they were no use and so I smashed them to pieces.
>
> (Watson, 34)

16   Yao or Shun: mythic rulers (reigns 2357–2255 and 2255–2208 B.C.) who came to be deified. Their names call up the Golden Age of China.

29   Ch'ao and Yu: paradigmatic recluses who lived during Emperor Yao's reign. He offered the throne to each of them; each refused and hurried away to wash his ears clean.

39   Hua-ching Palace, the emperor's mountain resort, was on Tu's route.

40   Ch'ih Yu banners: Ch'ih Yu was an infamous rebel who tried to overthrow the mythic emperor Huang Ti and was defeated in 2698 B.C. Ch'ih Yu banners carried an image of Ch'ih Yu and were used to chase away demons. For Tu, it must have been clear by now that the outbreak of the An Lu-shan rebellion was imminent.

43   Jasper Lake: the palace hot spring. Hsi Wang Mu (p. 154), queen of the Taoist immortals, lives in a palace at Jasper Lake in the mythic K'un-lun Mountains. Tu Fu uses this name with considerable sarcasm.

64   *Koto:* I use *"koto"* to translate *"ch'in"* and *"se,"* two

similar instruments which are the *koto's* Chinese an-
cestors.

100 South Mountain: see p. 136.

CH'ANG-AN II

MOONLIT NIGHT

5–6 This is perhaps the first Chinese poem to address such
romantic sentiments to a wife (it is especially striking
here because the poem is a *lü-shih*). The tropes Tu uses
to describe his wife had often been used to describe cour-
tesans and court women, the conventional objects of such
romantic feelings.

CH'EN-T'AO LAMENT

T Ch'en-t'ao: site just west of Ch'ang-an where a large im-
perial army suffered a disastrous defeat on November 17.
The army, which was under the command of Fang Kuan,
had been sent to recapture the capital.

SPRING LANDSCAPE

5 Beacon-fires: In times of war, neighboring garrisons
would light beacon-fires each night at the same time to
signal one another that they were still secure.

ABBOT TS'AN'S ROOM, TA-YÜN MONESTARY

T In an untranslated poem, Tu Fu says he is hiding in this
large Zen monestary to avoid being forced into service
for the rebel government.

7 Jade String: a constellation in our Ursa Major.

8 Temple phoenix: The temple roof was apparently deco-
rated with a large iron phoenix—perhaps a type of
weather vane.

P'ENG-YA SONG

T This poem recounts the flight of the Tu family from Feng-hsien to Fu-chou just after the rebels captured Ch'ang-an. They made their journey, which was about 140 miles long, in 756, one year prior to the poem's composition.

32   It was generally thought that the soul left the body when a person was surprised or frightened.

35   It was also thought that in sleep the soul drifted away (p. 142).

JADE-BLOSSOM PALACE

T   These ruins were on the route from Feng-hsiang to Fu-chou. Tu Fu's journey along this route is recounted in "The Journey North" (31). As Tu knew well, this palace was built by Emperor T'ai-tsung, the founder of the T'ang Dynasty, who used it to escape the summer heat in Ch'ang-an.

6–7   Earth's ten thousand airs: the music of earth, as opposed to the music of man (that played at the palace in its days of splendor, e.g.). It is described in *Chuang Tzu* 3/2/3:

> The Great Clod belches out breath and its name is wind. So long as it doesn't come forth, nothing happens. But when it does, then ten-thousand hollows begin crying wildly. Can't you hear them, long drawn out? In the mountain forests that lash and sway, there are huge trees a hundred spans around with hollows and openings like noses, like mouths, like ears, like jugs, like cups, like mortars, like rifts, like ruts. They roar like waves, whistle like arrows, screech, gasp, cry, wail, moan, and howl, those in the lead calling out *yeee!*, those behind calling out *yuuu!* In a gentle breeze they answer faintly, but in a full gale the chorus is gigantic. And when the fierce wind has passed on, then all the hollows are empty again. Have you never seen the tossing and trembling that goes on?
>
> (Watson, 36–7)

THE JOURNEY NORTH

T   This is the inner section (lines 19–92) of an unusually long poem, a little more than half of its 140 lines. This inner section is framed by rather courtly accounts of the circumstances surrounding Tu's journey and his vision of the dynasty's future return to glory. The journey from Feng-hsiang to Fu-chou, where he had left his family in Ch'iang Village, was about 215 miles long. Tu was only able to acquire a horse at Pin-chou, so the first third of his journey was on foot.

1   Heaven and Earth: *Ch'ien-k'un*, the cosmological manifestations of the principles *yang* and *yin*, whose interaction makes up occurrence, the process of change. Often translated as "the universe."

25   Peach Blossom: T'ao Yüan-ming's classic fable, "Peach Blossom Spring," tells of a fisherman who discovers a secluded farming village, unknown to the outside world, where people live in peace and contentment, untroubled by the world's concerns.

31   Owls call: The owl's voice resembles that of a ghost or spirit; so, when it calls, it is thought to be calling the spirit of a dying person away.

35   T'ung-kuan Pass: where the armies defending Ch'ang-an suffered their disastrous defeat in 756 (p. 121)—not actually on Tu Fu's route.

38   Ch'in: p. 135.

MEANDERING RIVER

1.5 The palatial homes in Meandering River Park (p. 136)
−6   would have been one of the first targets for rebel plundering when the capital fell. The park itself was neglected and little-used at this time.
     Unicorns: One of China's four great mythical animals, unicorns (*ch'i-lin*) appear only in times of benevolent rulers and great sages. Stone unicorns were placed beside tombs to protect the dead from evil.

2.1 Because the rebellion had exhausted the government's resources and destroyed its tax base, it could only afford to pay its officials irregularly.

DREAMING OF LI PO

3 Li Po had become involved, perhaps unwittingly, with the leader of a minor rebellion in the southeast. Once the rebellion had been put down, Li was banished to a waste region in the far southwest—an exile few survived.

7 Spirit: It was widely believed that the soul could leave the body during sleep and when a person is frightened or surprised (pp. 29, 50). So long as the person is alive, the soul is quite restricted in its movements. The soul of a dead person, on the other hand, has complete freedom of movement, even over vast distances, hence Tu Fu's worry.

FOR THE RECLUSE WEI PA

2 Scorpio and Orion: One of these constellations sets just before the other rises, so they never "see" each other.

THE CONSCRIPTION OFFICER AT SHIH-HAO

8 Yeh: the city where loyal armies had recently suffered a devastating defeat (p. 124).

PARTING IN OLD AGE

T For the *yüeh-fu* speaker, see p. 135.

CH'IN-CHOU/T'UNG-KU

CH'IN-CHOU SUITE

1.2 Wei Hsiao: a first-century warlord and inveterate rebel.

3.1 K'un-lun: a mythic mountain range in the far west where the Taoist queen of the immortals (Hsi Wang Mu— p. 154) lives.

3.3 Ch'iang: one of the Tibetan tribes near Ch'in-chou which had ostensibly submitted to the T'ang government.
Wu's envoy: The Han Emperor Wu sent Chang Ch'ien to find the source of the Yellow River. According to one legend, he sails to Hsi Wang Mu's palace. Another version of the story has it that he eventually finds himself on

the Celestial River (Milky Way), which is the empyrean continuation of the Yellow River (p. 152).

MOONLIT NIGHT THINKING OF MY BROTHERS

2   Goose: a conventional symbol for autumn and letters from loved ones far away.

3   White Dew: the two-week period following the Mid-Autumn Festival.

AT SKY'S-END THINKING OF LI PO

7   Ill-used ghost: Ch'ü Yüan (343–278 B.C.), China's first great poet. An admirable minister and patriot in the southern state of Ch'u, Ch'ü Yüan was slandered by members of the court and, as a result, banished. He became the archetypal exile for scholar-officials, who inevitably compared themselves to him when they suffered the very frequent sentence of banishment themselves. His exile caused him such grief that he eventually drowned himself in the Mi-lo, a river in the Tung-t'ing Lake region where Li Po was at the time. The legend of Ch'ü Yüan survives in the *Ch'u Tz'u* (*Songs of the South*), an anthology of poems which is one of the two landmarks of ancient Chinese poetry.

STAYING THE NIGHT WITH ABBOT TS'AN

T   Tu Fu's note: "Exiled, the abbot of Ch'ang-an's Ta-yün Monastery is peacefully settled here." See p. 27.

THE NEW MOON

5   Heaven's River: the Milky Way.

POUNDING CLOTHES

T   This *yüeh-fu* ballad is surprising because it is a *lü-shih*, the most literary of forms.

2   Fulling-stones: To make clothes, women would full cloth by beating it on a stone with a stick or mallet. When it appears in poetry, fulling cloth generally indicates a

woman's longing for a distant lover (the man for whom the clothes are being made), no doubt because of the act's unmistakable eroticism. It is usually linked with autumn and war because fulling heavy cloth to make winter clothes for soldiers fighting on the frontier was a kind of grief-filled autumn ritual for the women who were left alone at home.

SEVEN SONGS AT T'UNG-KU

1.1   Tzu-mei: Tu Fu's literary name.

1.3   Tsu the monkey sage: an allusion to *Chuang Tzu* 5/2/37:

> But to wear out your brain trying to make things into one without realizing that they are all the same—this is called "three in the morning." What do I mean by "three in the morning?" When the monkey trainer was handing out acorns, he said, "You get three in the morning and four at night." This made all the monkeys furious. "Well, then," he said, "you get four in the morning and three at night." The monkeys were all delighted. There was no change in the reality behind the words, and yet the monkeys responded with joy and anger. Let them, if they want to. So the sage harmonizes with both right and wrong and rests in Heaven the Equalizer.
>
> (Watson, 41)

1.7   These songs are all in the standard, 8-line ancient-style form. However, the seventh line of each song has an extra character added—a significant breach of form.

4.1   Chung-li: a district just south of the Huai River, which flows east through Anhui.

5.8   Soul gone: cf. pp. 142, 157.

6.1   Dragon: In Chinese mythology, the dragon descends into deep waters in autumn. It hibernates there until spring, when it rises and ascends into the sky. The dragon embodies the spirit of change, that is, of life itself, so its awakening is equivalent to the awakening of spring and the return of life to the earth.

This poem also contains a political allegory which is dependent upon its more basic mythological structure. The snakes represent the rebels, who came from the east, and the dragon represents the emperor. With the coming of spring, then, the dragon would rise and destroy the snakes.

6.5 This couplet recalls a story in *Han Shu* (*History of the*
–6 *Former Han Dynasty*) IA:6b–7a. In the story, Kao-tsu, who was to become the first emperor of the Han Dynasty, was traveling through some marshes when he encountered a huge snake blocking the road. He bravely drew his sword and cut the snake in two. Kao-tsu's victory symbolically prophesied the victory of the Han over the Ch'in. In Tu Fu's mind, the T'ang Dynasty was always linked to the great Han.

7.1 Another breach of form occurs here, where Tu has added two characters at the beginning of the song's first line.

CH'ENG-TU

ASKING WEI PAN TO FIND PINE STARTS

T Pine: Because they are large, strong, and ever green, pines represent permanence and constancy, a stoicism which perseveres under the harshest conditions.

FOUR QUATRAINS

2.1 Cloud . . . rain: induced by dragons which have become
–2 active and risen from the bottom of the stream where they had been hibernating.

3.4 Wu: the coastal region where the Yangtze flows into the sea, once controlled by the ancient state of Wu.

4.4 The healing effects of medicinal herbs and roots were thought to derive from their resemblance to other things in shape. For example, ginseng was thought to resemble the form of human beings, hence its power to promote longevity.

THE PLUM RAINS

T   The plum rains arrive each year when the plums ripen, in late spring or early summer, depending on the location.

1   Southern Capital: Ch'eng-tu had been declared the Southern Capital because Emperor Hsüan-tsung went into exile there when the rebel armies captured Ch'ang-an.

A GUEST

2   *Ch'i*-sited: The site for a new house would be chosen with the help of a diviner who used a divining rod and a special type of astrological compass. It was thought that the different features of a landscape determine the movement of *ch'i*, the universal breath or life-giving principle. A site would be chosen by determining how a family's particular characteristics (in this case, a leading consideration was Tu's health problems) harmonized with these movements. The Chinese word for asthma (*huan-ch'i*) literally means "afflicted *ch'i*."

A FARMER

7   Ko-hung: p. 134.

8   Cinnabar: the principle ingredient in the legendary elixir of immortality. This red, naturally occurring substance is rich in mercury, which explains the often lethal effects of such elixirs.

THE FARMHOUSE

8   Cormorants: Unlike most waterbirds, cormorants have no oil glands, so they spread their wings to dry them in the sun. As the people of this region used trained cormorants for fishing, their presence is perhaps a comfort for Tu—an image of the tenuous security his impoverished family has found. But at the same time, these large black birds cannot help but recall the frightening crows which keep reappearing in Tu's poems (one Chinese name for the cormorant is *"shui-lao-ya,"* "old water crow").

A MADMAN

2 Angler of Ts'ang-lang: a sagely, reclusive fisherman who
drifts calmly with the process of change. See "The Fisher-
man" ("*Yü Fu*") in the *Ch'u Tz'u* (p. 143).

OUR SOUTHERN NEIGHBOR

1 Chin-li: Brocade District, the area around Ch'eng-tu.

THROUGH CENSOR TS'UI I SEND A QUATRAIN TO KAO SHIH

T Kao Shih: the eminent poet whom Tu Fu met with Li Po
in 744. Also exiled with the Fang Kuan circle, Kao was
serving as prefect nearby.

MORNING RAIN

5–6 Huang and Ch'i . . . Ch'ao and Yu: unregenerate re-
cluses who wouldn't trade away their solitude even when
offered the nation. The former date from the second/
third centuries B.C. For the latter two, see p. 138.

SPRING NIGHT, DELIGHTED BY RAIN

8 City of Brocade Officers: The brocades made at Ch'eng-tu
were once so prized by China's emperors that they ap-
pointed brocade officers in the city to preside over the
work.

TWO IMPROMPTUS

1.6 Master of cap-strained wine: T'ao Yüan-ming (p. 137),
who was famous for his love of wine. Being poor, he
strained homemade wine through his cap.

2.7 Tu Fu's note: "He is a recluse in the Eastern Mountains."
O-mei, one of those mountains, is southwest of Ch'eng-tu.

FOUR RHYMES AT FENG-CHI POST-STATION:
A SECOND FAREWELL TO YEN WU

T Yen Wu: pp. 126–27.

WAYHOUSE

5   This line is a highly condensed variation on *Tao Te Ching*,
    27: "The enlightened one, ever masterful at saving peo-
    ple, abandons no one, and ever masterful at saving things,
    abandons nothing."

9/9, ON TZU-CHOU CITY WALL

T   9/9: p. 137.

FAREWELL AT FANG KUAN'S GRAVE

T   Fang Kuan: Tu Fu's friend and political patron, and one
    of the preeminent statesmen of the age. The previous
    November, returning from exile (p. 123), he died while
    staying at a monastery near Tzu-chou.

5   Hsieh An: a highly cultivated recluse (320–385) who re-
    luctantly entered government service. His armies fought
    a decisive battle which would determine the fate of China.
    The outcome was anxiously awaited by everyone, but
    Hsieh was playing *go* when news of a sweeping Chinese
    victory arrived, and it is said that he continued playing
    without any sign of emotion.

6   Hsü: On a diplomatic mission, Chi Cha (6th c. B.C.)
    visited the king of Hsü. When the king admired his
    sword, Chi Cha decided to give it to him after completing
    his mission. When he returned, however, he found that
    the king had died, so he hung the sword beside the king's
    grave as an offering.

SIX QUATRAINS

T   In addition to being highly integrated thematically and
    imagistically, this sequence is unified by following the
    course of a single day from morning until night, a day
    punctuated in section 4 by a violent thunderstorm.

K'UEI-CHOU

CH'U SOUTHLANDS

T Ch'u: The region Tu Fu is now entering was once controlled by Ch'u, the ancient state Ch'ü Yüan served.

IMPROMPTU

2 Second watch: There were five watches in the night, two hours each, beginning at 7 p.m. and ending at 5 a.m.

K'UEI-CHOU'S HIGHEST TOWER

5 Great Mulberry: The sun is, according to myth, ten crows —one for each day of the week. Each day, one sun-crow rises from the Great Mulberry (*fu-sang*) in the far east. After setting, it waits in the branches of this tree until its turn to rise comes again, ten days later.

6 Jo River: a mythic river of ether-like liquid where the sun goes down in the far west.

7 Goosefoot: a shrub with leaves that resemble goose feet.

BALLAD OF THE FIREWOOD HAULERS

16 Chao-chün: Wang Chao-chün (Wang Ch'iang) was a legendary beauty of the Han Dynasty.

8-PART BATTLE FORMATION

T 8-Part Battle Formation: a group of large megaliths standing in the Yangtze near K'uei-chou. Although they probably date from very ancient times, legend had it that Chu-ko Liang (181–234) built them during a military expedition against the state of Wu which ended disastrously for his forces. Chu-ko Liang was a paradigmatic scholar-recluse turned state minister.

BALLAD OF THE ANCIENT CYPRESS

1 It was believed that Chu-ko Liang had planted this cypress himself, so a temple was built beside it in his honor.

8 Snow Mountains: a range in western Szechwan.

9   Brocade Pavilion: the pavilion Tu Fu built at his hermitage in Ch'eng-tu.
10   Near Ch'eng-tu there was a temple devoted to both Chu-ko Liang and the king he served so well, which apparently had two large and ancient cypresses on its grounds.
16   Creation: p. 133.

SKIES CLEAR AT DUSK
1   Failing flare: literally "return shine" (*fan-chao*), that time shortly after the sun sets, when the colors return for a last few minutes with their greatest intensity.

OVERNIGHT AT THE RIVERSIDE TOWER
8   Heaven and Earth: p. 141.

NIGHT
4   Fulling-stick: pp. 143–44.
5   This is Tu Fu's second autumn in the south.
5   Geese: p. 143.
7   Cowherd: Altair (p. 155).
     Northern Dipper: our Big Dipper.
8   Silver River: the Milky Way.
     Phoenix city: an honorific name for China's capital, implying that a benevolent and wise ruler is on the throne there (the mythic phoenix appears only in times of peace and sagacious rule).

BRIDAL CHAMBER
4   Dragon Lake: part of the Hsing-ch'ing Palace complex in eastern Ch'ang-an.

REFLECTIONS IN AUTUMN
"Reflections in Autumn" is frequently nominated as the greatest poem in Chinese literature. Leaving aside concerns of content, the poem's achievement lies in its symbolist poetics; its calculated use of syntactic ambiguity (it contains the first instance of this in the Chinese tradi-

tion); its profound and sustained complexity; and its innovative form: the lyric sequence.

The poem's meditation moves between two halves of a dichotomy, each of which includes many closely interrelated elements. On the one hand is K'uei-chou. The elements included here are: present; reality; immediate perception; fact; mortality; insecurity; poverty; war; disorder; absence of civilization; the deteriorated contemporary T'ang Dynasty (as opposed to the splendid pre-rebellion T'ang of Tu Fu's earlier life at the capital); the T'ang Dynasty (as opposed to the Han which was, in Tu Fu's mind, the pinnacle of Chinese civilization).

Occupying the other half of this dichotomy is Ch'ang-an, the capital. The elements included here are: past; dream/imagination/reminiscence; desire; myth; immortality; home; security (court appointment); prosperity; peace; order; civilization; the pre-rebellion T'ang Dynasty (as opposed to the deteriorated contemporary T'ang); the Han Dynasty, which also had Ch'ang-an as its capital, especially Emperor Wu's reign (as opposed to the T'ang).

Although at least some attention is directed toward each half of the dichotomy in every poem, in the first three poems it is centered in K'uei-chou (these poems form a progression from evening to the following morning). Poem 4 is transitional. And in poems 5–8, it is centered in Ch'ang-an, although it is always heavily weighted with irony, and the imaginative energy which carries it there inevitably collapses in the final couplet.

For a close reading of this difficult poem (and the Chinese poetic language itself), see Mei Tzu-lin in the bibliography.

1.2   Wu Gorge: the second of the three awesome gorges which begin at K'uei-chou. Here, as is often the case with Tu Fu, the term refers to Three Gorges as a whole.

1.5   This is Tu's second autumn in the south.

2.3   Gibbon's voice . . . : from an old fisherman's song:

Three gorges east of Pa—Wu Gorge the longest.
After a gibbon's third cry, tears stain my clothes.

2.4 September raft: After flowing out to sea in the east, the
Yangtze and Yellow Rivers ascend and rarify, becoming
the Celestial River (Milky Way). The Celestial River
crosses the sky, then descends in the west to form the
headwaters of the Yangtze and Yellow. The September
raft refers to an empty raft that floated past the home of
a Yangtze fisherman every September. The fisherman,
thinking this strange, boarded the raft one year. He drifted
downstream and out to sea. For the first ten days, the
sun, moon and stars appeared normal. Then they grew
indistinct, as did night and day. After another ten days,
he came to a city where he saw a girl weaving cloth in a
palace and, across the river he realized he was on, he saw
a young cowherd watering his cows. When he asked the
girl where they were, she gave him the shuttle from her
loom and told him to show it to Yen Chün-p'ing who
would answer his questions. The fisherman left and, some
time later, arrived in Szechwan (hence he is returning to
China from the west). There he found Yen Chün-p'ing, a
famous astrologer. Yen identified the shuttle and told the
fisherman that he had seen a wandering star come be-
tween Weaving Maid and Cowherd (Vega and Altair, on
opposite sides of the Celestial River—p. 155) for one
night. The date which he gave for this celestial event co-
incided exactly with the fisherman's discovery of the weav-
ing girl and the cowherd. The same legend is told of Chang
Ch'ien (p. 142), who was sent by the Han emperor Wu to
find the source of the Yellow River. After sailing far up-
stream, he also found himself on the Celestial River, en-
countering a nearly identical sequence of experiences,
although he returned back down the Yellow River to
Ch'ang-an. In one version of this story, Chang Ch'ien
sail as far as the palace gardens of Hsi Wang Mu (p. 154).
This double allusion mirrors the poem's interest divided

between K'uei-chou (Yangtze River) and Ch'ang-an (Yellow River).

Stray journey: Tu Fu calls his journey "stray" because he has gone nowhere and, unlike the mythic travelers, he will never return.

2.5 Incense and ministerial portraits: Incense was burned to scent the robes of officials serving in the Department of State Affairs (*shang-shu sheng*) at the capital, where portraits of eminent statesmen hung. When he served as a military advisor in Ch'eng-tu, Tu Fu was connected to a branch of this department.

3.5 K'uang Heng . . . Liu Hsiang: K'uang's admonitions and
–6 Liu's devotion to scholarship were highly valued by their Han emperor. Quite the opposite was true for Tu Fu. In sum, the Confucian order had collapsed.

3.8 Five Tombs: built in Ch'ang-an during the Han Dynasty to honor five valiant heroes.

4.1 Chessboard: Ch'ang-an is compared to a chessboard because of the many armies that had recently fought back and forth across the checkerboard grid of its streets (and perhaps also because little besides that grid remained of the city). Very similar to western chess, Chinese chess represents a battle between two armies (the king's Chinese counterpart is a general).

4.5 Gongs and drums: Gongs were used by the military to sound retreat, drums signaled attack.

4.6 Feathered messages: Urgent messages were marked with a feather.

5.1 The first three couplets of this section are a nostalgic
–4 recreation of dynastic fortune at its height (in the Confucian order, a rich and peaceful court would be synonymous with a rich and prosperous country). But at the same time, the first two couplets are a kind of dreamscape (leading into the dream-like memory of Tu's life at court in the third) filled with supernatural scenes associated with the unsavory Taoist pursuit of immortality. Emperor Hsüan-tsung became obsessed with this pursuit, and his obses-

sion is usually given as one of the principle reasons for the T'ang's collapse. Commentators see in Hsi Wang Mu an allusion to the other reason: Hsüan-tsung's favorite concubine, Yang Kuei-fei.

P'eng-lai: P'eng-lai Palace, part of the emperor's palace complex in Ch'ang-an, which was named after the island of the immortals in the Eastern Sea (p. 134).

South Mountain: in terms of esoteric Taoism, a symbol of longevity (cf. p. 136).

Gold stalks: statues of immortals holding pans to collect dew. They were built in Ch'ang-an by Emperor Wu. Dew is one of the principle ingredients in the elixir of immortality, which is central to the Taoist endeavor.

Hsi Wang Mu: queen of the immortals and a central figure in Taoist mythology. She lived in a palace on Jasper Lake (p. 20) among the peaks of the mythic K'un-lun Mountains in the far west. She controlled the constellations, and the fabulous gardens of her palace produced the magic peaches of immortality.

Purple mist: According to Taoist mythology, purple mist accompanied Lao Tzu on his journey west out of China. In the tradition of the esoteric school of Taoism, Lao Tzu was on his way to Hsi Wang Mu's palace. However, Lao Tzu's journey introduces a complicating counterpoint here: according to the folklore of philosophic Taoism, the Taoist tradition which Tu Fu took seriously, Lao Tzu left China in despair at the ways of men, a sentiment very much present in "Reflections in Autumn."

6.1 Ch'ü-t'ang Gorge: the first of the Three Gorges, beginning at K'uei-chou.

Meandering River: p. 136.

6.3 Calyx Tower: part of Hsing-ch'ing Palace, on the eastern edge of Ch'ang-an, which was connected to Meandering River Park by a private arcade. Quite enthralled with Yang Kuei-fei and the Taoist pursuit of immortality, the emperor withdrew into this complex and began neglecting state affairs, a self-indulgence which soon led to disaster for China.

Frontier grief: the grief caused by the wars which were being fought at the time.

6.4   Hibiscus Park: Meandering River Park, where the emperor conducted lavish entertainment on land and afloat.

6.7   Land of song and dance: borrowed from the concluding lines of "Chant for White Hair," a long lament on the fleeting nature of life by Sung Chih-wen (d. 712):

> And of ancient, enduring lands of song and dance, nothing
> Beyond brown twilight in sight, and twittering sparrow
>   sorrows.

6.8   Ch'in: the Ch'ang-an region (p. 135).

7.1   K'un-ming: lake built near Ch'ang-an as a training site for Emperor Wu's naval forces.

7.3   Weaving Maid: For the Chinese, the story of Weaving Maid (Chih Nü) and her husband, Cowherd (Ch'ien Niu), is one of the most familiar myths. They are identified as stars facing one another across the Celestial River—Vega and Altair, respectively (with two small stars beside Vega as their twin children). In one version of the myth, Weaving Maid lived beside the Celestial River, where she wove the cloth of sky with its pattern of clouds. Her father arranged her marriage to Cowherd, who lived on the opposite bank of the river. Once they were married, however, the lovers were so entranced with one another that the girl neglected her weaving. Consequently, she was sent back to her loom. Since then, the two have been allowed to meet only one night each year, on the 7th day of the 7th month, when magpies form a bridge across the river. When forced to part at the end of the night, they weep bitterly, which is why there are heavy rains in autumn. Another version of this legend has it that Weaving Maid is the granddaughter of Hsi Wang Mu, and that Hsi Wang Mu created the Celestial River to separate the two lovers.

Statues of Weaving Maid and Cowherd stood on opposite sides of K'un-ming Lake, thus making it a kind of man-made Celestial River.

7.4   Stone whale: There was a stone whale in the lake which was thought to embody the spirit controlling storms and winds. When the scales of this "whale" shook, it was supposed to augur disaster. In the poem, this statue has ominously usurped the place of Weaving Maid's husband.

7.5   Zizania: *ku-mi*, a close relative of North American wild rice.

8.1   In his years at Ch'ang-an, Tu Fu frequented these famous
−2   places.

8.3   These two lines are equally contorted in the original.
−4

8.7   Florid brush: When he was young, Chiang Yen (443–504) had a dream in which he was given a pen that produced flowers. From then on, his writing was far more elegant than it had been before. Ten years later, in another dream, the pen was reclaimed and Chiang Yen's writing began to fail. *Chiang Yen* literally means "river" + "tarry" or "drown."

DAWN AT WEST TOWER, FOR YÜAN

4   Jade String: constellation (p. 139).

NIGHT AT THE TOWER

4   River of stars: one more appellation for the Milky Way.
7   Chu-ko Liang: p. 149.
    Pai-ti: first-century founder of K'uei-chou. In stark contrast to the impeccable Chu-ko Liang, Pai-ti was an infamous minister turned rebel and warlord.

RIVER PLUMS

1   La Festival: The earliest celebration for the New Year, the La Festival falls about two weeks before the lunar New Year.

TWO QUATRAINS

T The two sections can be read as a single 8-line poem.

3 These swallows would be gathering mud for their nests.

LATE SPRING

2 Hsiao and Hsiang: the region south of Tung-t'ing Lake, named after two of its major rivers. Tu Fu had often hoped that he could travel to this region and settle there.

FAILING FLARE

T Failing flare: p. 150.

8 Unsummoned soul: While Tu Fu is thinking of his being "unsummoned" to the court, he is also alluding to lines 23–29 of the "Summons of the Soul" (from the *Ch'u Tz'u*—p. 143), where a shaman-speaker is trying to recall the soul of Ch'ü Yüan after he has died:

> O soul, come back—you cannot stay in the south.
>   There, tattoo-faced and black-toothed,
> they offer human flesh to gods and pound bones into paste.
> Deadly cobras are everywhere there; huge thousand-mile foxes roam.
>   And nine-headed monsters
> flash near and far feeding their heart's content on people.
> O, come back, come back—you'll never last long there.

THE MUSK DEER

T Musk deer: very small animals, averaging only two feet in height, and very timid. Today, musk deer *(chi)* are slaughtered in the wild by the hundreds of thousands not for food, but for their musk oil (each male having only one teaspoon of oil), which is used in fine perfumes.

3 Hermit immortals: After studying for many years, a Taoist hermit named Ko Hsien-weng became an immortal and was transformed into a white musk deer.

DAY'S END

7–8 Flame flickers good fortune: It was thought to be an auspicious sign when a lamp's flame sputtered.

AUTUMN PASTORAL

This sequence resumes the innovations of "Reflections in Autumn."

1.3   Well Rope: the star which, according to Chinese astrology, controls the fortunes of the K'uei-chou region.

2.8   North Mountain's ferns: Po Yi and Shu Ch'i (12th c. B.C.) were esteemed recluses who lived at the end of the Shang Dynasty. Although the Shang emperor was frightfully malevolent, they refused to change their allegiance when the dynasty was overthrown. Refusing even to eat the grain of the benevolent new Chou Dynasty, they withdrew to North Mountain, where they lived on ferns until they finally died of cold and hunger. A bitterly self-mocking allusion.

3.1   Paraphrasing Confucius and Chuang Tzu, line 1 proposes
−3   the Confucian way (in terms Chuang Tzu specifically denounces), line 2 the Taoist one.

3.3   Gauze cap: These caps, made of thin black silk, were worn by officials. The neglected state of Tu's cap suggests that he has let his Confucian discipline go by the boards. The rest of the poem confirms him as a follower of the Tao.

4.6   Ch'ing-nü: a goddess who controls frost and snow. She brings frost in the third month of autumn.

4.8   Southern Palace: a constellation. It was also a name for the Department of State Affairs, to which Tu Fu had been appointed when he served as military advisor in Ch'eng-tu. At night, white quilts were given to the officers serving in this department at the capital.

5.1   Unicorn portraits: p. 135.

5.7   Hao Lung (4th c.) served in this region as Military Ad-
−8   visor under a particularly pugnacious and infamous minister. He once used the local aboriginal dialect in a poem and, when questioned, bitterly replied that his language couldn't help but be barbaric now that he was serving in such a distant, barbaric place.

ASKING OF WU LANG AGAIN

T   Wu Lang: Tu Fu's nephew, who was staying in the guest-house at Tu's Nang-west estate.

6   Tax . . . : These oppressive taxes were levied to support the huge armies needed to defend the country.

GONE DEAF

1–2   Ho Kuan, Lu P'i Weng: famous recluses from ancient times.

4   Deaf as dragons: Dragons cannot hear. The character translated by this phrase, *lung* ("deaf"), is made up of two elements: "dragon" + "ear," a good example of the immediacy and evocative richness which characterizes Chinese semantics.

5   Autumn tears . . . gibbon's cry: pp. 151–52.

THOUGHTS

2.15   Knotting ropes: a method of calculation and record-keeping which preceded written language in pre-history.

LAST POEMS

RIVERSIDE MOON AND STARS

2   Jade String: constellation (p. 139).

4   Strung Pearls: the five planets which the Chinese knew: Mercury, Venus, Mars, Jupiter, and Saturn.

CHIANG-HAN

T   Chiang-han: "Yangtze and Han," the region where the Yangtze and Han rivers converge.

2   Heaven and Earth: p. 141.

FAR CORNERS OF EARTH

5   Wang Ts'an: Han Dynasty poet who, under circumstances similar to Tu Fu's, fled from Ch'ang-an to the semi-

barbaric Yangtze plains, where Tu Fu was when he com-
posed this poem.

6   Ch'ü Yüan: pp. 143, 149.

DEEP WINTER

4   Yang Chu: a shadowy proto-Taoist philosopher (4th c.
B.C.) whose sayings are recorded in the *Lieh Tzu*. He
once wept at a fork in the road because he knew either
choice would only lead to another fork, with the result
that he would become more and more lost.

5   Ch'ü Yüan's wandering soul . . . : The "Summons of the
Soul" was thought to be an attempt to call Ch'ü Yüan's
soul back to his body after he had died (p. 157).

SONG AT YEAR'S END

2   Hsiao and Hsiang: the region south of Tung-t'ing Lake
(p. 157).

5–6   In all standard editions, this couplet appears as lines 9–10.
But the incongruity that placement causes in the poem's
development is entirely resolved by advancing the couplet
to this position.

ON YO-YANG TOWER

2   Wu and Ch'u: regions once controlled by the ancient
states of Wu and Ch'u (pp. 145, 149).

4   Day and night: Like Heaven and Earth (p. 141), day and
night are manifestations of *yang* and *yin*.

OVERNIGHT AT WHITE-SAND POST-STATION

T   Tu Fu's note: "I have just passed 5 *li* beyond the lake's
southern shore."

5   *Ch'i*: the life-giving principle or universal breath.

6   Wandering Star: The raft upon which Chang Chien and
the fisherman (p. 152) floated to the Celestial River ap-
pears in the sky as the Wandering Star.

8   Southern darkness: from the fable which opens the
Chuang Tzu (1/1/1/):

In the northern darkness there is a fish and his name is K'un. The K'un is so huge I don't know how many thousand *li* he measures. He changes and becomes a bird whose name is P'eng. The back of the P'eng measures I don't know how many thousand *li* across and, when he rises up and flies off, his wings are like clouds all over the sky. When the sea begins to move, this bird sets off for the southern darkness, which is the lake of Heaven.

(Watson, 29)

FACING SNOW

7   Floating-ant wine: Expensive wine was fermented in silver jars covered with cloth. In the process, a layer of scum formed on top. When this worthless layer was skimmed off and sold to those who could afford nothing better, it was called "floating-ant wine."

A TRAVELER FROM

2   Mermaid pearl: It was believed that pearls grew from the tears of mermaids. Guangdong, on the southern coast, was China's chief source of pearls.

MEETING LI KUEI-NIEN SOUTH OF THE RIVER

T   Li Kuei-nien: a renowned opera singer. He was by now old and sorrowful, much like Tu Fu, having been driven south by the wars.

ENTERING TUNG-T'ING LAKE

T   This poem was found in the middle of the Hsiang River, engraved on a large rock where the river flows into Tung-t'ing Lake, and later attributed to Tu Fu.

2   White-Sand: p. 160.

THOUGHTS, SICK WITH FEVER ON A BOAT

1–4   By playing musical instruments which they had invented, the mythic emperors Huang Ti and Shun created order and harmony on earth.

9   Ma Jung's flute: After several years away, Ma Jung heard

a flute song he had once listened to in the capital. This filled him with sorrow and longing for his home there.

10   Tunic . . . Wang Ts'an: Wang Ts'an (p. 159), longing for his home at the capital in the north, wrote: "I face into the north wind and open my tunic." A particularly apt allusion, because the wind from "a cold homeland" might help cool Tu Fu's fever.

17   Ghosts . . . drums: Local tribes used drums to summon ghosts.

18   Owls: p. 141.

The poem continues for another fifty lines, as the fever falls through Tu Fu "like mountain cascades," modulating into a drifting review of his life and the political situation. But that section is less compelling poetically, and the density of its allusion precludes successful translation.

FINDING LIST

Texts:

1. Kuo, Chih-ta. *Chiu-chia chi chu Tu-shih.* In William Hung's *A Concordance to the Poetry of Tu Fu.* (*Chüan* and poem number)

2. Yang, Lun. *Tu-shih ching-ch'uan.* (*Chüan* and page number)

Poems can be located in other standard editions by using the finding list in volume 1 of Hung's *Corcordance,* pp. cxiii–cxci. To locate the poems in Erwin von Zach's complete German prose translation, *Tu Fu's Gedichte,* see von Zach's finding list (pp. 810–864).

Page	1. Chiu-chia chi chu Tu-shih	2. Tu-shih ching-ch'üan	Page	1. Chiu-chia chi chu Tu-shih	2. Tu-shih ching-ch'üan
xvii	2/11	2.28b	25	19/6	3.18b
3	1/5	1.1a	25	2/22	3.17b
3	1/4	1.1a	26	19/5	3.18b
4	17/14A	1.2a	26	19/9	3.20a
4	18/2	1.3a	27	19/10	3.21a
5	17/17	1.9b	27	2/19A	3.23a
9	18/7	1.5a	28	3/19	4.8b
10	1/12	1.21a	30	3/6	4.3a
11	5/15	2.3b	31	3/3	4.4b
14	18/22	1.25a	34	19/30	4.17b
15	2/3	2.1b	35	5/10A	5.22a
16	2/9	2.29b	35	1/20	5.7b
17	1/24	2.23a	36	3/11	5.16b
18	1/16B	2.24b	37	3/13	5.17b
18	2/16	3.8a	41	20/1B,D,	

Page	1. Chiu-chia chi chu Tu-shih	2. Tu-shih ching-ch'üan	Page	1. Chiu-chia chi chu Tu-shih	2. Tu-shih ching-ch'üan
	J,Q	6.1a	68	7/6	7.29a
42	20/2	6.5b	69	26/13	11.36a
43	20/25	6.6a	69	24/47	10.19a
43	20/3	6.6b	70	26/25	12.4a
44	20/5	6.9a	75	27/26	12.18a
44	20/6	6.9b	75	27/25	12.25b
45	20/9	6.10b	75	31/44	12.28a
45	20/11	6.11a	76	13/14	12.31a
46	20/13	6.11b	76	31/7	12.28b
46	20/26	5.11b	77	7/10	12.30a
47	20/34	6.15a	78	29/14	13.13b
47	20/28	6.15b	78	30/2	13.17a
48	6/16	7.6b	79	31/4	13.29b
53	22/43	7.18a	79	31/2	13.31a
53	26/26	12.5a	80	30/8	17.6b
54	21/4	7.19b	80	31/38	14.3a
54	21/8	7.20a	81	31/39	14.3b
55	21/15	7.21a	81	30/32	13.22b
55	21/5	7.20a	84	31/19	15.9b
56	21/11	7.21a	85	31/43	15.10a
56	21/12	8.13b	85	33/8	15.19b
57	21/7	7.20b	86	25/23	11.24a
57	21/21	7.27a	86	28/11	15.22a
58	7/15	8.19a	87	32/25	15.24a
58	21/23	7.27b	87	28/3A	15.25b
59	22/22	8.10a	88	28/22	14.6a
59	21/46	8.4a	88	28/18	16.1a
60	23/3	8.11a	89	28/9	16.14b
61	23/5	8.5a	89	30/23B	16.17a
62	22/2	8.4b	90	29/28	17.10b
63	22/18	8.12a	90	31/35	17.11b
65	23/21	9.13b	91	30/6	14.4b
65	24/25	9.19b	91	29/23	17.13a
66	24/7	9.20a	92	30/29	17.15b
66	24/27	10.8a	92	32/29	17.16a
67	25/30	11.16b	93	29/19	17.16a
67	21/25	7.29b	93	30/37	17.17a

Page	1. Chiu-chia chi chu Tu-shih	2. Tu-shih ching- ch'üan	Page	1. Chiu-chia chi chu Tu-shih	2. Tu-shih ching- ch'üan
94	32/3	17.18a	106	30/16	19.11a
94	26/39		107	25/19	19.11b
	(30/50E)	17.19a	107	35/1	19.19b
95	30/34	17.1a	108	31/15	19.19a
97	28/25	17.20a	108	15/12	19.20b
97	32/4	17.27a	109	35/4	19.22a
98	32/18A	17.28a	109	35/9	19.24a
98	32/28	17.33b	110	36/9	20.15b
99	32/12	17.34a	110	15/4	20.16b
100	13/19	18.4a	111	15/7	20.17a
102	13/29	18.13a	111	34/12	20.25b
105	27/10	12.11b	112	36/27	20.33a
105	34/5A	19.4a	112	36/12	20.34a
106	34/6	19.4b			

BIBLIOGRAPHY

I. EDITIONS OF TU FU'S POETRY

Ch'iu, Chao-ao. *Tu-shih hsiang chu.* 1713. The most thoroughly annotated edition.

Kuo, Chih-ta. *Chiu-chia chi chu Tu-shih.* 1181. In Hung, William. *A Concordance to the Poetry of Tu Fu.* Harvard-Yenching Institute Sinological Index Series, Supplement, no. 14. 3v. Beijing, 1940. Taipei reprint, 1966. The standard edition of the text.

Yang, Lun. *Tu-shih ching-ch'uan.* 1791. The most serviceable and widely available edition, with poems arranged in generally accurate chronological order. Based on Ch'iu's edition.

II. TRANSLATIONS AND STUDIES

Alley, Rewi. *Tu Fu: Selected Poems.* Beijing: Foreign Language Press, 1962.

Ayscough, Florence. *Tu Fu: The Autobiography of a Chinese Poet, Volume I, A.D. 712–759.* Boston: Houghton Mifflin, 1929.

————. *Travels of a Chinese Poet: Tu Fu, Guest of Rivers and Lake,* Volume II, A.D. 759–770. Boston: Houghton Mifflin, 1934.

Birch, Cyril, ed. *Anthology of Chinese Literature.* 2 v. New York, Grove Press, 1965.

Cheng, François. *Chinese Poetic Writing.* Bloomington: Indiana Univ. Press, 1982.

Chuang Tzu. *The Complete Works of Chuang Tzu.* Trans. Burton Watson. New York: Columbia Univ. Press, 1968.

Ch'ü Yüan. *Ch'u Tz'u, The Songs of the South.* Trans. David Hawkes. London: Oxford Univ. Press, 1959. Penguin reprint, 1985.

Cooper, Arthur. *Li Po and Tu Fu*. Hammondsworth: Penguin Books, 1965.

Davis, A. R. *Tu Fu*. New York: Twayne Publishers, 1971.

Graham, A. C. *Poems of the Late T'ang*. Hammondsworth: Penguin Books, 1965.

Hawkes, David. *A Little Primer of Tu Fu*. Oxford: Clarendon Press, 1967.

Hung, William. *Tu Fu: China's Greatest Poet*. Cambridge: Harvard Univ. Press, 1952.

Liu, Wu-chi and Irving Yu-cheng Lo, eds. *Sunflower Splendor: Three Thousand Years of Chinese Poetry*. Garden City: Doubleday, 1975.

Mei, Tsu-lin and Kao Yu-kung. "Tu Fu's 'Autumn Meditations': An Exercise in Linguistic Criticism," *Harvard Journal of Asiatic Studies*, 28 (1968), 44–80.

Owen, Stephen. *The Great Age of Chinese Poetry: The High T'ang*. New Haven: Yale Univ. Press, 1981.

Rexroth, Kenneth. *One Hundred Poems from the Chinese*. New York: New Directions, 1971.

Seaton, J. P. and James Cryer. *Bright Moon, Perching Bird: Poems by Li Po and Tu Fu*. Middletown: Wesleyan Univ. Press, 1987.

Shih Ching. The Book of Songs. Trans. Arthur Waley. London: Allen & Unwin, 1937.

T'ao Yüan-ming. *The Poetry of T'ao Ch'ien*. Trans. James Hightower. Oxford: Oxford Univ. Press, 1970.

Von Zach, Erwin. *Tu Fu's Gedichte*. Cambridge: Harvard Univ. Press, 1952.

Watson, Burton. *Chinese Lyricism: Shih Poetry from the Second to the Twelfth Century*. New York: Columbia Univ. Press, 1971.

————. *The Columbia Book of Chinese Poetry: From Early Times to the Thirteenth Century*. New York: Columbia Univ. Press, 1984.

Yoshikawa, Kojiro. "Tu Fu's Poetics and Poetry," *Acta Asiatica*, 16–17 (1969), 1–26.

Young, David. *Wang Wei, Li Po, Tu Fu, Li Ho: Four T'ang Poets*. Oberlin: FIELD Translation Series, 1980.

INDEX OF TITLES AND FIRST LINES

Poem titles are printed in *italic* type.

169

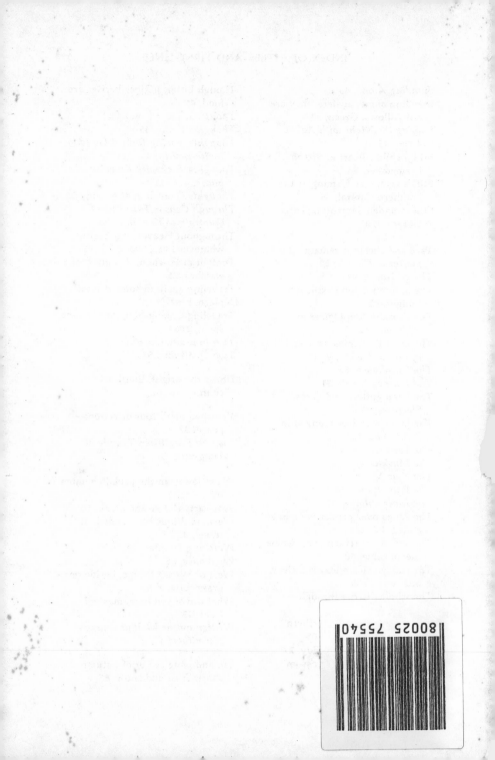